Extreme Mind Makeover

Learn more about this book and its
author by visiting our web site:

www.overboardministries.com

ISBN:0983456828
ISBN-13:978-09834568-2-7

Cover design by Innovative Graphics
www.igprodesign.com

This title is available for your favorite eReader. Visit
our web site to choose the format
that's right for you.

All comments or requests for
information should be sent to:
overboard@overboardministries.com

All Scripture quotations, unless otherwise indicated, are taken from the
Holy Bible, New International Version®. *NIV*®. *Copyright* © 1973, 1974,
1984 by International Bible Society. Used by permission.

References followed by "KJV" refer to the King James Version of the
Bible.

DEDICATION

It was Fall of 2003 and I had baggage — lots of it. Emotional, psychological, spiritual, you name it. Having chosen to live in sin for over 30 years, the ramifications of those choices were finally catching up with me. No matter how hard I tried to keep things together, my life was falling apart. To the world around me I appeared to be "normal." In fact, I was considered a spiritual leader in the church. Yet inside…well, let's just say I was a miserable wreck.

My wife and I had already seen three different counselors, but nothing seemed to be helping. Then God led a man from our church into my life. This man didn't sit there and judge me as I shared my sinful past. He didn't lecture me; pointing his finger at me, telling me that I was a horrible sinner — I already knew that. No, he patiently sat with me week after week and shared God's Word with me.

He challenged me, encouraged me, prayed with me, wept with me, and loved me. Through his ministry I began to realize that God truly loved me for who I was, and that He hadn't abandoned me. God still had a plan for me. With this man's help I discovered that Scripture not only exhorts, it encourages, heals, helps, and gives hope.

Soon his wife and mine joined in the weekly meetings. Not all of them were enjoyable. There were times where we walked away from a meeting angry and frustrated. Never because of what this couple said or did, but because the Holy Spirit was using God's Word to chip away at our heart issues. Yet we always came back. They were always there. They never faltered in sharing God's truth with us. That truth, coupled with the wonderful work of the Holy Spirit in our hearts, changed us — both of us.

Today, as a result of investing a year of their lives into ours, my wife and I share a husband-wife relationship that is stronger than it has ever been. Our walk with God continues to grow. Our family and friends continue to notice a significant change. We are now counseling others with the same truth — God's truth — that had been shared with us. This book is a direct result of the ministry of **Roger and Carol Cryan** in our lives. Today they are our dearest friends. We thank God for them.

Thank you Roger and Carol for allowing God to use you.

CONTENTS

TESTIMONIALS

You might be wondering how this book can really help you. How can the changing of your thought life make a real difference? I have studied under this man of God. I know his heart to help you — as he helped me — see that God is a jealous God. God wants us to love Him with all of our heart, mind, and soul — Luke 10:27. But do we really?

If you take the time to read this book and apply it to your life, you will find that you will want to become more like Christ and glorify Him forever. I wish that someone had pointed out these truths to me at a much earlier age. I challenge you to allow this book and the truths inside to assist you to become the person Jesus Christ wants you to be.

John M. Swart

* * * * *

Having made a personal profession of faith in Jesus Christ early in life, we have completed multiple organized group and independent Bible studies. Completing the *Extreme Mind Makeover* study forced us to look at personal battles between the spiritual nature and the sinful fleshly desires we struggle with.

This study showed us that we are not to passively wait for spiritual growth to occur but we are to be actively engaged and pursuing it. Steve uses multiple Biblical references to support these principles, making it a welcome consideration of the individual "metamorphosis" that should be transforming our Christian walk.

We are thankful to Steve for bringing this thought provoking study on controlling our minds in order to direct our hearts and transform our lives.

Larry & Lori Dooley

* * * * *

I was privileged to participate in the *Extreme Mind Makeover* class Steve taught regarding the choices we make in our lives and what we can do to better insure they are the right ones; the ones that honor our Heavenly Father.

Satan can no longer impact our souls once we have accepted Christ as our Savior, but he sure knows how to attack our minds. One of the things Steve taught that will stay with me is that "what we think becomes what we do." To make sure we do the right things, we need to change the way we think. I know *Extreme Mind Makeover* will help guide you through God's Word to a better way of thinking.

Bill Douglas

* * * * *

I so enjoyed walking through Scripture with Steve, and being impacted by his life experiences. Through his examples, and more importantly through Scripture, I've been able to see how important it is to be immersed in the Bible. I learned how our human nature wants to be driven by our feelings and emotions.

While they have a place in our lives, "feelings" can often lead us to make wrong choices. *Extreme Mind Makeover* leads you systematically through the Scriptures, showing you how the battle in your life is for your mind. As one song put it years ago, "Love is a Battlefield." In *Extreme Mind Makeover* you will discover that the more accurate line should be, "The mind is a battlefield." One saying *Extreme Mind Makeover* drives home is from Scripture, and I paraphrase, "What a man thinks, so is he."

This book shares many Scripture verses that discuss how important of a role the mind plays in our lives; the one that stands out to me the most is Romans 12:2a: *"Do not be conformed to this world, but be transformed by the renewal of your mind..."* (ESV). It would have been so helpful to me years ago to have been shown the concept of "renewing my mind" through Scripture. This is something that should be taught in schools, not just at church...

Scott Mitchell

* * * * *

Extreme Mind Makeover is not a book about theory, but about the practical application of God's truth in Steve's own life and how it helped him overcome a "habit" of sin. In this book he shares with the reader the lessons he learned and he helps the reader understand how he or she can apply those powerful, biblical lessons in their own life!

Carl Reichanadter

ACKNOWLEDGMENTS

I did a little research, just out of curiosity, to see what the word "acknowledgement" actually means. After all, it only makes sense that I should know what I'm writing about. Here's what I learned: to acknowledge is to admit to something. It is an expression of appreciation in recognition of the importance or quality of something.

How very apropos then, to use that term to identify this section. I definitely want to admit to knowing the people mentioned below (as to whether that feeling is mutual remains to be seen) because they have had tremendous impact in my life. It is because of that impact that I want to mention them specifically. This is an expression of my appreciation for their involvement in my life.

First is my wife, **Heather**. She loved me when I was unlovable. She believed in me, fought for me, and stayed by my side when I was at my worst. I love you sweetheart and thank God every day for the blessing and honor of being your husband. Thank you for not giving up on me. And thank you for tolerating the long hours of being alone while I focused my attention on this book.

Second, I want to acknowledge our children **Andrew** and his wife **Catey**, **Philip**, **Bekah** and her husband **Ben**, and **Elisabeth**. Kids, you've watched your dad agonize and battle with his sin issues. You have been witness to the miracle God has performed in my life. You've prayed for me, cried with me, laughed with me, and encouraged me to write this book. My deepest heart's desire is to always be a living example of what I have written within these pages. Thank you for allowing God to use you in my life.

Though he may not know it, the next person I want to acknowledge is a man for whom I have a deep, deep respect. He has modeled for me what it means to be a man of God. He has taught me from the Word. He has prayed with me, loved me, encouraged me and helped me see when I was wrong. He made a commitment to Heather and I 16 years ago that he would walk beside us through our journey of healing, and he has kept his word. Thank you **Pastor John Blodgett** for being you — a man totally surrendered to God.

Next, I want to thank **Pastor Dave Hills** and **Pastor Phil Byars** who have both been my long-time friends and accountability partners. Without their involvement in my life I wouldn't be where I am today. Gentlemen, for many years you met with me on a regular basis — holding my feet to the fire. You never gave up on me. You weren't afraid to ask the tough questions. The impact you have had in my life can never be measured. You've prayed for me, you've challenged me and encouraged me. You are the truest definition of "friend."

Finally I want to thank the countless number of people who have played an integral role in the development of this material. This includes my extended family that prayed for and encouraged me along the way and everyone who ever took my class and urged me to write a book about it. This section would not be complete without acknowledging my dear editor **Michelle McKinney** without whom you would be struggling to understand my thoughts, and my publisher **Joe Castañeda** — thank you Joe for seeing the vision and helping me tell others how to have an *Extreme Mind Makeover*!

Foreword

In 1996 a guy named Steve Etner began attending our church. As I got to know Steve it became clear that he desired, and needed, an accountability relationship. Together, with another man in our church, we began to interact on a regular basis. We would ask each other key questions about our personal disciplines, purity, integrity, family life, etc. In doing so, we were putting into practice the words of Proverbs 27:17, "As iron sharpens iron, so one man sharpens another."

Over the years since then I have had a "front row seat" to Steve's life. Beyond an accountability partner, Steve is a beloved brother, co-laborer, counselor, and friend. As a pastor, I am blessed to have a man with Steve's gifts, abilities, and passion serving alongside me in the teaching and counseling ministries of our church. It's always a good day when I can meet with Steve to talk "life" over a plate of wings.

What you will find in *Extreme Mind Makeover* is a book that comes straight from the heart of a man who has been genuinely transformed by the truth of God's Word. Thankful for what God has done in his own life, he has put on paper the principles that God used to radically change the way he thinks and lives. What I appreciate so much about Steve's life, and the book he has written, is the unapologetic, and uncompromising emphasis on the power of the Word of God *alone* to transform lives. He truly believes the precious words of 2 Peter 1:3-4:

> *"His divine power has given us everything we need for life and godliness through our knowledge of Him who called us by His own glory and goodness. Through these He has given us His very great and precious promises, so that through them you may participate in the divine nature and escape the corruption in the world caused by evil desires."*

God bless you as you read this book and, as my friend Steve so aptly puts it, "may your everyday living and your every-moment thinking be pleasing and glorifying to God." This book will help you to reach that goal.

Dave Hills
Discipleship Pastor
First Baptist Church – Bristol, IN

Introduction

It is life-changing when we discover that at the root of many of our problems is wrong thinking. Jesus said, *"Make a tree good and its fruit will be good, or make a tree bad and its fruit will be bad, for a tree is recognized by its fruit"* (Matt. 12:33). Your thoughts bear fruit: your behavior. When you think good thoughts, the fruit of your life — the things you do — will be good. Think bad thoughts, and the fruit of your life will be bad. When I first began to realize this truth in my life, it was hard at times to change my thinking patterns. God's Word teaches that our thought process (mind) must be renewed in order to live a transformed life that truly glorifies Him (Rom. 12:2). When we learn to change the way we think, we can know God more and enjoy the life God wants us to have — one of freedom, fruitfulness, peace, and joy.

This book is a direct result of the impact God's Word has had in my own life. I have had the wonderful privilege of being a child of God for more than 45 years. Yet, for over 30 of those years I lived a defeated life, choosing to stay enslaved to my sins. Often I would cry out to God, begging Him to give me victory over the sinful habits that plagued me, all the while continuing to live in my sin. Feeling that there was no way out, I was discouraged, depressed, moody, self-absorbed; and my family suffered tremendously because of it. My behavior continued on a destructive course, until one day when I chose to turn my back on God and my family, which eventually culminated in a failed attempt at suicide. But God had other plans. He led me to a godly man in our church who counseled me directly from the Word of God. Week after week we would sit together with our Bibles, opening the Scripture to plumb the depths of its truth.

The Holy Spirit used the Word to help me consider what I was thinking about. He showed me that my actions are a direct result of my thoughts. My problems were rooted in sinful thinking patterns that actually produced the issues I was experiencing in my life. The more I read the Bible, the more I came to know God and His Word; as well as what it means to yield to His strength and not trust my own. I was able to compare what was in *my* mind with the mind of God. As the Holy Spirit taught me to change my thinking patterns to be in alignment with the truths of Scripture, I began to see a change in my behavior patterns as well. And so did my family and friends.

This process taught me how important it is for us to grow in our knowledge and understanding of God's Word. We need to renew our minds with His Word, and then, submitting to the power of the Holy Spirit, use the weapons of Scripture to tear down the strongholds and every high and lofty thing that exalts itself against the knowledge of God. Because our thoughts affect what we do, it must be a priority in our lives that we think right thoughts.

Today, God has blessed my wife and I with a wonderful ministry in our church. We are privileged to counsel others, taking them into the Word, showing them the same truths that were shown to me. A couple of years ago, when God provided the opportunity for me to teach a 12-week course at our church on how the Word of God impacts our thinking, which in turn affects our behavior, I was tentatively excited. Here was an opportunity to share with others on a broader scale what God had been teaching me.

The Psalmist asked God to create in him a pure heart and renew a steadfast spirit within him. His cry was that God would restore the joy of salvation to him, and then he would be able to teach others the ways of the Lord (Ps. 51:10-13). My heart's desire was — and still is today — to teach others, from God's Word, the things the Holy Spirit has revealed to me. To that end, I compiled a study that was focused entirely on Scripture. This book is the result of that journey.

As you work your way through this book, you will notice that I only quote one author: God. This is intentional because I want your focus to be entirely on what God has to say. Together we are embarking on a journey that is going to take us through the Bible to see what God has to say about the way we think and how we behave. We will be building on foundational blocks, using repetition, restating a biblical principle in a number of different ways, and viewing it from different angles — even looking at the way the passage was written in the original language for greater clarification. This is geared to help you understand the precepts in God's Word and discover how they apply to your everyday living.

I have personally found that when reading a book that makes a statement, and then quotes a verse to back it up, I will tend to skip over the verse. That is why you will find many of the verses we study together are actually woven into the flow of the sentences and paragraphs of this book. I am a firm believer in the importance of being in the Word of God. Therefore, each chapter is full of Scripture, integral to our understanding of the mind and the will of God. The foundation of this study is built upon the truths of God's Word. I don't want you to skip over God's Word so that you can read my words. God's words are far better!

I have also noticed that sometimes Christians will read a passage of Scripture yet not really consider what it is they are reading. The verse may be familiar, so they don't think about what the verse is saying or how it applies to them. As we read God's Word we need to ask: What do I need to do in my life as a result of this Truth? As you read this book, I encourage you to slow down and read at a pace that enables you to absorb the truths and principles of Scripture. Pray over them. Memorize them. And most of all, live by them.

There were times in my life as I was fighting this battle over the thoughts in my mind when I felt it was impossible, I just couldn't do it. I would wonder where God was in my struggles. Then the Holy Spirit would remind me that *"when you pass through the waters, I will be with you; and when you pass through the rivers, they will not sweep over you. When you walk through the fire, you will not be burned; the flames will not set you ablaze"* (Isa. 43:2).

At the end of his search he makes this one, final, powerful declaration, *"Now all has been heard; here is the conclusion of the matter: Fear God and keep His commandments, for this is the whole duty of man"* (Eccl. 12:13). This is what Solomon is saying, "I've searched long and hard, far and wide, trying to find meaning and purpose to life and I've come to a conclusion: Meaning and purpose to life is found only when I embrace that God is good and wants His best for me; when I acknowledge that He is powerful and holy, and, therefore, worthy of my respect and obedience. This is my primary desire and pursuit; it is what I was created for."

That affirmation is just as true for us today as it was for Solomon. We were created for one purpose alone: to know God and live a godly life that brings honor and glory to Him in everything we say and do (Isa. 43:7; 1 Cor. 10:31; Col. 3:17). True purpose and meaning to life cannot be found in fame or fortune, people or pleasures. The obtaining of a sense of significance comes only as you fulfill the intent of your creation — discovering an intimate, personal relationship with God and walking in obedience to His commands.

King David wrote in Psalm 112:1 that the man who fears the Lord and delights in His commands is blessed of God. In other words, when you are doing that which God created you to do, you are truly happy. God commands each of us to *"fear the LORD your God, to walk in all His ways, to love Him, to serve the LORD your God with all your heart and with all your soul, and to observe the LORD's commands and decrees...for your own good"* (Deut. 10:12-13; cp. 1 Sam. 15:22; Prov. 21:3; Mark 12:29-31). It could not be more clear. A life lived in pursuit of bringing glory to God and pleasing Him will be characterized by godliness. When you walk in humble obedience to God, bringing glory to your Father, Savior, and Friend — as you were created to do — you are fulfilling your purpose and that is when you will find lasting joy, peace, and meaning in life!

The question you must face here is this: Do you truly *want* to live a life that consistently glorifies God? I mean, deep down in your heart of hearts do you want, long, desire, or crave for a life characterized by godliness? Let's assume, for the moment, that your answer is, "Yes. I want to live a life that in every way reflects God. I want to daily be, think, do, say, and feel in the ways God wants me to." My question for you then is this: What are you doing right now to achieve that goal? What plan of action do you have in place to pursue that purpose? As the saying goes, there's no better time than the present!

Simply wanting something isn't going to make it happen. For example, I want to be 20 pounds lighter, but unless I change my daily life habits and consistently adhere to a specific diet and exercise program, losing that weight isn't going to happen. In fact, if I'm not careful just the opposite could happen. I want to be a godly man, but unless I make some spiritual lifestyle changes and adhere to a specific spiritual "diet and exercise program," it will not happen. To be godly you must have a plan and actually put it into motion. So again I ask you, what are you doing right now to pursue godliness?

We must understand that godliness does not automatically happen for the Christian. The moment you were saved you did not become instantly godly. Nor does godliness come easy. Take a close, hard look at your spiritual life to date. Have you periodically tried to be godly only to find that you failed in your attempts? Why do we seldom succeed even when our desires are genuine and our efforts are sincere? After all, we definitely want to do the right thing. We want to glorify God in our daily lives yet we tend to fall short of our goal

Divinely Equipped

The person who is training to run a marathon not only sets up a plan on how to achieve their goal, they also surround themselves with the right equipment necessary for the task. Proper running shoes, the right kind of clothes that fit comfortably and breathe, possibly a treadmill and an elliptical machine are all things a serious runner wants to consider. In the same way, if we are going to train ourselves to be godly, we need the right equipment.

In his second epistle, Peter writes, *"(God's) divine power has given us everything we need for a godly life through our knowledge of Him who called us by His own glory and goodness"* (2 Pet. 1:3 NIV). Wow! Did you catch that? God provides *everything* we need to live a godly life through our knowledge of Him.

There's a lot of truth packed into this verse and if we are going to be successful in living a life that glorifies God, we need to dig it out! First of all, notice that it is God's divine power that provides us with everything we need to live a godly life. By using the word "divine," Peter is telling us that which is being spoken of (namely, the power to be godly) belongs to God alone. Only God possesses the ability to provide all that we need to live godly lives. That power does not naturally reside within you; it does not naturally reside within me. In and of ourselves we will always fail to be godly, which is why it is divine. With that in mind, let's take a closer look at that word "power." It refers to the *natural capability* to do something. The one who has this kind of power is not dependent upon an outside source to accomplish the task. The power or ability resides completely within the individual. So "divine power" means that only God has within Himself the capability of equipping you and me with everything we need to live a godly life.

We must consider this carefully. You and I cannot manufacture godliness on our own. Job asks the question, *"Who can bring what is pure from the impure?"* He then answers, *"No one"* (Job 14:4). In and of ourselves, we are incapable of being godly. In fact, God says, *"All have turned aside, they have together become corrupt; there is no one who does good, not even one"* (Ps. 14:3; cp. Ps. 53:3; Rom. 3:10-12). *"All of us have become like one who is unclean, and all our righteous acts are like filthy rags; we all shrivel up like a leaf, and like the wind our sins sweep us away"* (Isa. 64:6; cp. Isa. 53:6). Ecclesiastes 7:20 says, *"There is not a righteous man on earth who does what is right and never sins."*

We are incapable of being godly. The only way we can live a life that glorifies God is if God Himself, who has that power naturally, comes to dwell within us — placing His own

4

godliness within us through His Spirit, and we, in turn, learn how to yield to His power. Peter assures us that God's divine power has given the believer everything we need for a godly life.

Don't miss Peter's use of the words "has given." God's divine power *has given* us everything we need. That phrase is written in the perfect tense, passive voice. When something is written in the perfect tense, it describes an action which is viewed as having been completed in the past, once and for all, never needing to be repeated again. By writing that God's divine power *has given* us everything we need in the perfect tense, Peter is saying that this has already been done for us. It does not need to be repeated ever again. As a born-again believer, you already have everything you need to live a godly life — you don't have to ask for it — because God's divine power has already been given to you.

Furthermore, when something is written in the passive voice, it means the subject is the *recipient* of the action as opposed to being the *doer*. In other words, it has been done to or for you and not *by* you. Here is where it gets exciting — we are the subject of this verse. God's divine power has given *us* everything we need. Every person who names the name of Jesus Christ as Savior is the *recipient* of everything we need to be godly.

Now consider this: God's divine power has given you *everything* you need. The word "everything" is literally the word "all." I once heard a preacher say that "All" means all and that's all "all" means! I like that. It is a word that refers to each and every part of the whole, leaving absolutely nothing out. God's divine power has given you *all* you need for a godly life. That's fantastic! You cannot manufacture it on your own, but you don't need to. You already have it. All of it! You don't have to go looking anywhere else for it. God has already given it all to you.

come simply from having head knowledge of the Scriptures. You can know a lot of Biblical truths and principles; you can have a lot of passages memorized and know Bible doctrine. But if you are not living those truths out in your daily life, if you are not living by the doctrine you know to be true, you are not glorifying God — you are not a godly man or woman. Period.

Peter says that God's *"divine power has given us everything we need for life and godliness through our knowledge of Him who called us by His own glory and goodness"* (2 Pet. 1:3). Since God has the ability to help me glorify Him, and my godliness comes only as I gain knowledge of Him, the key then to being godly is to understand what Peter means when he speaks of "knowledge." The word Peter uses is *epignosis*, a word that refers to a thorough participation on the part of the knower (you), with the object of knowledge (God); a knowledge that has a powerful and lasting influence on the knower. In other words, the *knowledge* you have of God is so precise and clear that you are now able to fully comprehend it. It is no longer just a vague grasp of the subject; rather it is thorough and exact.

The end result of this kind of knowledge is a change in the way you think. Because you now know it and understand it, you think about it differently. Since your thinking has changed, there is a subsequent change in your behavior. What you think becomes what you do.

God has given you everything you need to live a godly life, and it comes only as you grow in your knowledge — a deep understanding — of Him. As this happens, you will begin to think about Him differently. Since your thinking has changed, your behavior will be different because of what you now know to be true about God. You will begin living out godliness.

In addition, to have the kind of knowledge Peter is talking about in this verse requires an intimate experience with that which is being known. It is not a surface knowledge. Nor is it a head knowledge that involves knowing a bunch of facts. It goes much, much deeper. For example, I will never be able to say, "I know Abraham Lincoln." I may have accumulated a vast amount of information about him, and can give you all sorts of interesting tidbits about his life and leadership but I do not know him. At best I can say I know *about* him. To truly know him, I would have had to live during his lifetime, spent every day of his life under the same roof observing and conversing with him. That intimate experience would give me a precise, clear, and exact knowledge of the man, Abraham Lincoln. Only then could I say that I know him.

I do, however, have a clear and precise knowledge of my wonderful wife, Heather. Because I have lived with her for over 30 years. Because I have observed and experienced first-hand the things that interest her, excite her, upset her, motivate her, and inspire her, I can say that I truly know her. And as a result, that knowledge has a direct impact upon my life.

What I know to be true about Heather has changed the way I think about her. That, in turn, has changed the way I respond to her. I have grown to love her and long to please her. The knowledge I have accumulated over the years has had a powerful impact upon me, teaching me how to live my life in such a way as to keep her interest, excite her, keep her from being upset, and motivate and inspire her toward a closer walk with God.

The Book of Books

Peter is saying that a deep, intimate understanding of God is how we acquire everything we need to live a godly life. And yet, in Job 36:26, we read these words: *"How great is God — beyond our understanding! The number of His years is past finding out."* Scripture declares that God is beyond our ability to know; we cannot be thoroughly acquainted with Him. To make things even more interesting, when Job said that God is beyond our understanding, he used the imperfect tense. The imperfect tense expresses that which is incomplete and is not possible to ever complete. This means that, apart from God's divine intervention — which He offers through His own Spirit — man's knowledge of God is, and always will be, incomplete and thus imperfect.

"Can you fathom the mysteries of God? Can you probe the limits of the Almighty? They are higher than the heavens — what can you do? They are deeper than the depths of the grave — what can you know? Their measure is longer than the earth and wider than the sea" (Job 11:7-9). Job 37:23 says, *"the Almighty is beyond our reach."* Paul says that God is *"...the blessed and only Ruler, the King of kings and Lord of lords, who alone is immortal and who lives in unapproachable light, whom no one has seen or can see"* (1 Tim. 6:15-16). The bottom line is that it is impossible to know God on our own. In fact, Romans 3:11 tells us that there is no one who seeks after God on their own. Add to that the fact that man is a sinner and we see that it becomes absolutely necessary that if God is to be intimately known, He must be the one to start the process.

We can positively conclude that He did that, otherwise Peter would be lying as he says, *"God's divine power has given us everything we need for a godly life through our knowledge of Him"* (2 Pet. 1:3 NIV). God has revealed something of Himself to us through the Bible. As a result, we can intimately know our Creator and Father — because He has given us His Spirit to teach us — as we read the Scripture. You see, the Bible is the very Word of God! Paul writes that *"all Scripture is God-breathed"* (2 Tim. 3:16). It came from the very mouth of the Almighty God Himself. And Peter tells us that *"men spoke from God as they were carried along by the Holy Spirit"* (2 Pet. 1:21). The purpose of this book is not to go into a theological discussion on the doctrine of Bibliology, but it is important to our study that we understand that the Bible is God's Word. It is God's revelation of Himself to man. To get to know the God of the Word you must be in the Word of God, for it is there that we discover who He is. And it is there that we find everything we need to live a godly life.

Furthermore, the Bible tells the truth, and it does so without error. Why is that so important? Consider this; if the Bible were to contain even just a few minor errors, we could never be sure that our understanding of God, Christ, Heaven, Hell, sin, and salvation is correct.

Jesus said, "*Man does not live on bread alone, but on every word that comes from the mouth of God*" (Matt. 4:4). If the Bible has even one error in it, no matter how minor, everything should be brought into question. The fact is, we live our Christian lives by *every word* that comes from God's mouth. If even one word of Scripture is in error, we shouldn't trust any of it! Do not fret. God is true. God breathed out the Bible, therefore the Bible is true. All of it!

So, if you are going to be serious about living a life that glorifies God — a life that deeply and intimately understands God, you need to roll up your sleeves, grab your shovel and pick axe, and begin digging into the Word of God. That is where you are going to find your answers (2 Tim. 3:16-17; Heb. 4:12). The Bible is the solid foundation upon which we must build godly lives.

Let's look at 2 Peter 1:3 again. "*His divine power has given us everything we need for life and godliness through our knowledge of Him who called us by His own glory and goodness.*" Only God can give you what you need to live a godly life that honors and glorifies Him. The exciting thing is that His power has already provided you with all that you need to live that godly life. And He provided it all within His Word — the Bible. You will find everything you need as you open God's Word, study it, and meditate on it. Then, as you grow in your knowledge of God and in an intimate relationship with Him, the Holy Spirit will teach you and help you learn how to live a life that truly glorifies Him, a life that is genuinely godly.

Dear Christian friend, God has given you a new mind, a new nature, and a new heart. You are fully equipped to live a godly Christian life. I submit that you need to quit trying to live the Christian life! You can't do it in your own power. None of us have the knowledge or ability to do it on our own. Only as we are yielded to and reliant upon the indwelling Holy Spirit, as He uses the Word of God to guide us, will we become godly men and women whose daily lives truly glorify our Lord.

way that you benefit from it. In other words, if you want to be a wise man or woman, if you want to build a godly life on a solid foundation, *you* must continuously hear God's Word and daily put it into practice. I can't do it for you and you can't do it for me. It is personal.

Finally, when something is written in the indicative mood it means that it is a statement of fact. There is no room for argument or debate. God said it and that's final. If you are going to be a wise builder, you will be continuously in God's Word, listening to what God has to say, learning what God's will is, and actively putting God's principles into play in your daily life.

If you are going to become a godly man or woman, living a life that truly glorifies God, it is vital that you see God's truth for yourself, within the pages of your own Bible. That is when you make it personal. And only when it is personal will you be able to build your own spiritual life upon the solid foundation of God's Word. When faced with the storms of doubt, anxiety, worry, fear, frustration, lust, pride, and so on, the only way you are going to be able to stand firm in the faith is if you have already been building your life upon the solid foundation of Scripture as you have personally studied (Ps. 119:11).

To say, "Well, my pastor said…" or, "I remember reading in such-n-such a book that…" or, "I heard the guy on the radio say…," won't hold up under the strain of the storm. But when you are able to say, "God says!" and quote God's promises directly from God's Word, you will be able to withstand the strongest of attacks because you have built your faith upon the solid foundation of God's Word. Building a godly life is all about God's truth found in God's Word showing us God's will for our lives, which in turn will equip us to glorify Him as we walk in obedience to His commands. As we will see later on, only the Word of God, through the work of the Holy Spirit, can accomplish genuine lasting change in our lives (Heb. 4:12). As you invest time in the study, memorization, and meditation of God's Word, seeking God through His Spirit for the integration of that Truth into your daily life, you will experience a godly life that honors and glorifies the Lord.

Truth? You *can* Handle the Truth!

Titus 1:1 tells us, *"the knowledge of the truth leads to godliness."* Focus for a moment on the word "truth." In John 18 we see that when Jesus was standing before Pilate, He is asked the question, *"Are you a king?"* Jesus responds by talking with Pilate about truth, to which Pilate retorts, *"What is truth?"* then turns and walks away (John 18:36-38). This is a question that has been plaguing man for centuries: What is truth?

Today, society tries to tell us that truth is subjective. Have you ever heard comments like this: "There is no such thing as absolute truth," or, "Different people can define truth in conflicting ways and still be correct"? The pervasive philosophy in the public at large these days is that truth is whatever you choose to believe.

God says differently. In John 17:17 Jesus firmly declares that God's Word is truth. Not "a truth" but *the* truth, absolute truth absolutely. King David writes in Psalm 119:42-44 that he trusts completely in God's Word, and then he calls God's Word the "word of truth." The Pharisees, religious men in Jesus' day who were knowledgeable in the Scriptures, said of Jesus that He spoke and taught what is right, teaching the way of God "in accordance with the truth" — a direct reference to the Scriptures (Luke 20:20-22). In short, there *is* such a thing as absolute truth. It is found in God's Word. Whatever God says *is* absolute truth.

The knowledge of truth leads to godliness. In order to be godly you need to know the truth, but not just any "truth" — God's truth. But what does it mean to *know* God's truth? Consider for a moment the word "knowledge." If you go to the dictionary you'll read that one achieves knowledge when they are aware of and familiar with something because they have experienced it to some degree. According to that definition, as long as I am aware that something exists and am at least somewhat familiar with it, I can say I have knowledge of it. Paul is not talking about that kind of knowledge in Titus 1:1.

The word Paul uses here for knowledge is *epignosis* (see our discussion on 2 Peter 1:3, Chapter 1), which simply means that this knowledge you have is not some vague grasp of the subject; rather it is thorough and exact. The end result of this kind of knowledge is a change in the way you think. Because you now know it and understand it, you now think about it differently. Since your thinking has changed, there is a change in your behavior because of what you now know to be true.

Think about this: *Knowledge of the truth leads to godliness.* The outcome of having a clear knowledge of God's truth is a change in your thinking, resulting in a change in your behavior, creating an overall shift in your life toward godliness. Look at this equation:

Knowledge of Truth = Change in Thinking = Change in Behavior = Godly Living

When we truly know and understand God's Word, it will have an impact on the way we think. What we think becomes what we do, so if there is a change in our thinking, there will be a change in our behavior. You will act upon what you know to be true. This change in your behavior results in living a godly life that glorifies the Lord.

Let's think about this in reverse: To live a consistent godly life you must change your behavior. To change your behavior you must change the way you think. To change the way you think you must be in the Scriptures gaining a deep knowledge of God's Word and His will. In addition, to have the kind of knowledge that Paul is referring to requires an intimate experience with that which — and Who — is being known. It is not a surface knowledge. It goes much deeper.

Consider Titus 1:1 again, *"the knowledge of the truth leads to godliness."* How does one gain clear and precise knowledge of God's Word? Do we need to go to seminary and get a doctorate in Theology? Are we to be completely dependent upon our pastor and teachers to provide us with the things we need to know? No. You must invest your personal time daily in the study, meditation, and memorization of God's Word, and listen to the Holy Spirit as He speaks God's truth to you. As you become more intimate with the Word of God, and thus the God of the Word, there is going to be significant impact on your life. That clear and precise knowledge you are gaining will impact your thinking — and thus your doing — which will lead you to godliness. Not only will you experience an increasing desire to please God, you are going to become more godly as you learn how to discipline yourself in such a way that your daily life truly glorifies Him.

In Colossians 3, Paul lays out some guidelines for living to glorify God. As "God's chosen people," we are to exhibit *"compassion, kindness, humility, gentleness and patience"* (v.12). We should *"forgive as the Lord forgave"* (v. 13) and love each other. He goes on to encourage us to *"let the peace of Christ rule in [our] hearts"* (v. 15) and *"let the word of Christ dwell in [us] richly"* as we spend time doing things with other Christians, such as *"teach and admonish one another with all wisdom, and as you sing psalms, hymns and spiritual songs"* (v. 16). Paul notes repeatedly that we should live with thankfulness and gratitude to God as we follow these guidelines. In fact, it is clear that whatever we do should be done in Jesus' name, while giving thanks to God (Col. 3:17). This kind of living glorifies God. When we praise Jesus, we bring God glory. When we are grateful and thankful to God, we bring Him glory.

In Colossians 3:17 Paul states that *"Whatever [we] do, whether in word or deed, [we are to] do it all in the name of the Lord Jesus, giving thanks to God the Father through Him [Jesus]."* Look carefully at the way this verse is written. There is no option here. Whatever you do, *do it* in Jesus' name. This isn't something that would be nice if we could accomplish more often than not in our lives. This is God's expectation of His children. Now think with me for a moment. According to this verse, e*verything* that you say and *everything* you do is to honor the name of Christ. Did you catch that? Not just some of the things you say and do, not even most of those things. Everything.

Let's pause and consider what we're reading. There are some important truths I do not want you to miss. Let's focus on Colossians 3:17 and meditate on it, asking ourselves: 1. What is this verse really saying? 2. How does it apply to me? 3. What do I need to do in my life as a result of the truths contained here? It is critical that we be wise builders, establishing our godly lives upon the solid rock. To do that, we need to not only hear God's Word, but put it into practice as well (Matt. 7:24-27).

Paul starts this verse by using the word "whatever." This word, as it is used here, refers to the total of each and every thing. In other words, nothing — not even a single part of a thing — is to be left out of this equation. When Paul says, "*Whatever* you do," he means exactly what it says. The words, "whatever you do, whether in word or deed," are telling us that each and every word we say, as well as each and every thing we do — all of it, every part of it — must be said and done to the glory of God. Remember, God's expectation is that we glorify Him in everything. If it isn't glorifying Him, it is sin.

How often do you closely examine your words and actions — before ever speaking them or doing them — to make sure that they all glorify God? Yet that is what we are commanded to do. As the peace of Christ rules in your heart, and His words richly dwell in you, each and every part of all the things that you say and all the things you do should be focused on glorifying God. If that sounds impossible I have great news for you — it's not! God, who cannot lie (Titus 1:2), promises us in Philippians 4:13 that we can do *all* things through Christ who gives us the strength. All things! What does "all" mean? "All" means all and that's all "all" means! That promise includes the ability to glorify God in every single word and deed.

What's in a Word?

Look again at our verse in Colossians 3:17 and let's break it down even further. Paul says, "*Whatever you do in word or deed.*" In this sentence "word" is referring not just to the actual vocabulary that comes out of your mouth, but includes the attitude or motivation behind each and every word you speak. Simply put, you must seriously reflect on what is in your heart as you speak (Luke 6:45). Reflect on the driving force behind every specific word you say. Reflect on the reason you are saying this specific word and formulating this specific sentence. Determine whether it is for your personal benefit or for God's glory.

tongue means you are disciplining yourself to be extremely careful about what you say. Every word is guarded and thought through before being spoken. You never allow whatever comes to mind to leave your mouth without first considering it carefully as to whether it will glorify God or not. You put a watch over yourself so that nothing escapes your lips unexamined. What you speak reveals what is in your thoughts and your heart. Remember the children's song, "Oh, be careful, little tongue, what you say?" To that I add: "Oh, be careful, little mind, what you think!"

Our words can deceive (Rom. 16:18; Eph. 5:6), they can persuade (1 Cor. 2:4; Col. 2:4), cause quarrels and controversies (1 Tim. 6:4; 2 Tim. 2:14), and can appeal to the desires of the flesh (2 Pet. 2:18). Timothy was commanded to set an example for the believers in his speech (1 Tim. 4:12). Jesus personally lived the perfect example for us. In 1 Peter 2:21-22 we learn that *"Christ suffered for you, leaving you an example that you should follow in His steps. 'He committed no sin, and no deceit was found in his mouth.'"* Each of these verses provides plenty of reason to examine our hearts and guard our words. Never forget that whatever you say should be said for the sole purpose of glorifying God. Period.

In Matthew 12, as Jesus addresses the heart of the Pharisees, He states, *"out of the overflow of the heart the mouth speaks"* (Matt. 12:34). Now think about that for a moment. Your words — *every word* — and the motivation behind each word, reveal what is in your heart. Your words are a direct result of what is going on in your thoughts. What you think will come out in what you say. The ppsalmistsalmist declares in Psalm 139:4 that *"Before a word is on my tongue you know it completely, O Lord."* In other words, before you even speak a word, it is in your heart, it is in your mind, and God already knows it. The prophet Isaiah said that the man whose mind is busy with evil will speak folly (Isa. 32:6).

You need to ask yourself — and answer honestly — this question: Does each and every word I speak and the motivation behind them bring glory to God? When I am speaking to my spouse, to my children, to my employer or employees, to my co-workers, to my family members, to my friends and neighbors, even to those annoying telemarketers, am I considering carefully everything I am saying to be sure each and every word is glorifying God? Since your words reveal what is in your thoughts, the real question is: Do your thoughts truly glorify God? What you think will be revealed in what you say.

What am I Doing?

In Colossians 3:17 we see that Paul goes on to say, *"whatever you do in word or deed."* Usually we think of a deed as something that we do. For example, we may think of a good deed as being something we do, like helping out in the nursery at church or going on a short-term mission trip with the youth group or raking the neighbor's leaves. It certainly can, and does, include those things, but that simple word, "deed," in Colossians 3:17 refers to so much more. A "deed" can be something as simple as crossing your arms to make a point or offering a friendly pat on the back for encouragement.

This is a very powerful word! It refers to each and every individual thing we do no matter how insignificant we may think it is. Even the raising of an eyebrow, the shrug of our shoulders, the glaring of our eyes, the nodding of our head, or a smile of encouragement is considered by Paul to be a deed that should be done in the name of Jesus Christ. In short, every aspect of your body language is considered by God to be a deed that should bring Him glory and accompany the actual physical activities and actions you do.

It is also important for us to realize that these deeds are not referring only to the ones seen by men. It refers to each and every deed — whether in public or in private. Even the things you do when you're all by yourself are to be done to the glory of God. 1 Samuel 2:3 tells us that *"the LORD is a God who knows, and by Him deeds are weighed."* Consider that verse carefully. God knows each and every one of your deeds, public and private. But this verse reveals something more, something much deeper.

God not only knows your deeds but the motivation of your heart behind each deed. What is the *real* reason you're doing this? God knows!

In Jeremiah 17:10 God says, *"I the LORD search the heart and examine the mind, to reward a man according to his conduct, according to what his deeds deserve."* Whoa… wait a minute, did you catch that? On the scales of God's justice your deeds are seriously considered, but God places more weight on your hearts' motivation, on the thoughts you were thinking as you did each deed. Look again at this verse. God searches your heart and *examines your mind*. Yes, your deeds are important to God, but even more so is the reason behind it — that which was going on in your thoughts as you did it. And He is not going to reward your deed, no matter how great it might be, if the thoughts and motivation behind it was wrong. What you think will become what you do. In order for your deeds and actions to glorify God, your thoughts must glorify Him.

Think about this. Just as with your words, your deeds reveal what is in your heart. Proverbs 23:7 says that *"as [a man] thinketh in his heart, so is he"* (KJV). In other words, what you think will eventually become what you do. That means your words and your actions are clear indications of what is in your heart. All anyone has to do is look at the things you do, and listen to the words you say, and they will know what your thoughts are about.

Can you say as the psalmist honestly did, *"Test me, O LORD, and try me, examine my heart and my mind"* (Ps. 26:2)? I hope so. Because He *can* see the heart. He loves you and His purpose in your life is to refine you. He reveals what needs to be changed through His Word by His Spirit. He wants you to choose things that bring Him glory. All in all, it is for your good that He sees your heart, that He tests it, because His desire for you is always and only for your good.

All Means What?

Look again at Colossians 3:17. *"And whatever you do, whether in word or deed, do it all in the name of the Lord Jesus, giving thanks to God the Father through Him."* Paul is saying that each and every thing you say, as well as each and every thing you do, is to be said and done in the name of Jesus Christ. They are to be said and done with the sole intent of glorifying God. To glorify God in *everything* you say and do you must first glorify Him in *everything* you think. Jesus put it this way, *"Love the Lord your God with all your heart and with all your soul and with all your strength and with **all your mind**"* (Luke10:27, emphasis mine).

You may be familiar with 1 Corinthians 10:31, but let's look at the words of this verse and consider them. Paul writes: *"So whether you eat or drink or whatever you do, do it all for the glory of God."* I'm sure you noticed some similarities between this verse and Colossians 3:17. Paul says that *whatever* you do, you are to do it *all* for God's glory. Now let me ask you a couple of simple questions. I know the answers are obvious, but humor me. How much of your life is to glorify God? All of it! How many of the things you say and do should glorify God? All of them! And "all" means all and that's all "all" means. You see, even the most mundane, routine, and "non-spiritual" things of life are to be said and done in a way that glorifies God!

Let me remind you that the foundation we are building our study upon is this: You were created to know God and live a godly life that brings honor and glory to Him in everything you say and do. That is the primary purpose of life and the way you find true joy. If God is to be glorified in your daily life, He must first be glorified in your thought life. I can't repeat that enough. To glorify God in your everyday living you must first glorify Him in your every-moment thinking. There is a primary connection between glorifying God in every thought you think and glorifying Him in every word you say and every deed you do. Reflect again on what Proverbs 23:7 says of man: *"As he thinketh in his heart, so is he"* (KJV). What you think will eventually become what you do. This point is critical. If you are going to *live* godly you must first *think* godly. Yet, too often we tend to disassociate the two and focus all of our attention on changing only our outward behavior. This divorce results in legalism as well as feelings of discouragement and defeat every time we fail in our pursuit.

Before we go any further in this book, let me encourage you that victory is possible! We do not have to live defeated lives. For years I focused all my attention on changing outwardly, trying to behave the way I thought I knew God wanted me to. During that part of my life I struggled with feelings of defeat and failure because I was constantly going through the cycle of sinning ==> confessing ==> sinning ==> confessing, only to turn around and walk right back into my sinful patterns again and again. I lived in discouragement, feeling crushed under the weight of my sinful habits.

No more! This book is a result of my personal journey through the Scriptures, learning that the sin we battle with is not stronger than God. The temptation that seemingly overwhelms you is actually powerless over you — you *can* live a consistent godly life! You can learn how to walk in true victory over sin and how to live a godly life that glorifies our Heavenly Father. The answer is found within the pages of God's Word. God shows us how!

~ Four ~
Understanding Sin

Have you ever sinned? I know… Silly question. However, if we are going to live lives that glorify God, it is important for us to understand the depths of this issue and how it applies to us. Romans 5:12 says, *"Therefore, just as sin entered the world through one man, and death through sin, in this way death came to all men, because all sinned."* Every one of us not only has sinned, but is a sinner. We battle with sin every day of our lives.

Psalm 14:3 says, *"There is no one who does good, not even one"* (cp. Ps. 14:1; 53:1, 3; Rom. 3:12). Consider for a moment the words "does good." To "do" refers to producing something completely on your own. And the word "good" is in reference to that which is excellent in God's eyes. Put them together and we see the Psalmist declaring that there is no one who is capable of producing that which is excellent in God's eyes completely on their own. Left to ourselves we will sin.

Paul declares in Romans 3:23 that *"all have sinned and fall short of the glory of God."* To know true victory in your life — to live a godly life that truly glorifies your Heavenly Father — you must begin with the acknowledgement that your tendency is to sin.

What is Sin?

If we are going to effectively pursue godliness, we must gain a proper understanding of sin. To do that, let's focus our thoughts on four specific questions. First, what is sin? In 1 John 5:17 we read that *"all wrongdoing is sin."* Think about that as I repeat it. All wrongdoing is sin. Ahhh, but there are many different standards today of what is right and what is wrong. If all wrongdoing is sin, then we must ask, "Wrongdoing according to whom?"

In the grand scheme of things, it is more important to know what God says sin is than what you or I think sin is. In the end, I will not stand before your judgment seat nor will you stand before mine. 2 Corinthians 5:10 tells us that *"we must all appear before the judgment seat of Christ, that each one may receive what is due him for the things done while in the body, whether good or bad."* There is a day coming when you and I will stand before God and answer for all our wrongdoings (as well as our right-doings). What matters then is God's definition of right and wrong and our obedience to it.

In both the Hebrew and Greek languages (the languages in which the Bible was written), the word "sin" means a failure to hit the mark because of disobedience. In 1 John 3:4 we read, *"Whosoever committeth sin transgresseth also the law: for sin is the transgression of the law"* (KJV). Focus your attention for a moment on that word "transgresseth." A transgression is a breaking or violation of an established law. It is doing the opposite of what is required. In short, it is disobedience.

All sin is wrongdoing according to God because sin is breaking God's law, going against God's perfect standards and refusing to obey God's commands. Simply put, when you violate the commands of Scripture, you are guilty of sin (Jas. 2:10). God's Word is absolute truth (John 17:17). Therefore, when you do anything against, or in opposition to, God's truth, you are transgressing His law and thus sinning.

It is important that we have an understanding of what God says sin is because that is going to help us understand what goes on in our minds. Sin is calling your own shots — living for "King Me." Sin is living as if there was no law — other than your own — requiring your obedience (1 John 3:4). Sin is reading God's truths in God's Word, and choosing not to do what God says (Matt. 7:24-27). Sin is in the nature of the heart. God says, *"The heart is deceitful above all things and beyond cure"* (Jer. 17:9). It doesn't matter how good you may be; trip up in just one point, no matter how small the offense, and you are guilty of breaking all of God's law (Jas. 2:10).

Ask yourself what prevents you from living a consistent godly life. The answer is sin! In order to learn how to live a life that glorifies God, we must first learn what keeps us from accomplishing that task, and what we need to do about it. We cannot understand the solution to the problem unless we first understand the problem itself. The whole premise of this book is this: To glorify God in our everyday living, we must first glorify Him in our every-moment thinking. We will never be able to understand God's remedy for our thinking process if we don't understand the reason why we struggle with our thoughts.

Romans 5:12 says, *"Therefore, just as sin entered the world through one man, and death through sin, and in this way death came to all men, because all sinned."* When Adam sinned, you and I were there. We inherited that original sin nature. This means it is easier to do wrong than it is to do right. Before becoming a Christian your natural tendency was to think selfish, sinful thoughts which always lead to selfish, sinful behavior.

Today, the world at large rejects the concept of sin. Because they reject sin, they have no true understanding as to why they are the way they are. Everything today is considered to be a "lifestyle choice." Hardly anything is considered to be sin anymore. It is no wonder that we struggle so much with living godly lives when the world's wicked philosophy is all around us, permeating almost everything we see and hear, and thus influencing how we think and behave.

Where Does Sin Come From?

Here is our second question: When you sin, where does your sin (wrongdoing) come from? I can remember many years ago there was a famous actor that coined the phrase, "The Devil made me do it!" It was meant to be funny and cute, but it truly expresses the mind-set so many have. Man refuses to take responsibility for his sin. It is far easier to blame someone else for our wrongs.

So where *does* sin come from? Does the Devil make us sin? No. Does God make us sin? Definitely not! God is *"a faithful God who does no wrong, upright and just is He"* (Deut. 32:4). Genesis 18:25 says that God, the righteous Judge of all the earth, does what is right. Job cried out, *"Far be it from God to do evil, from the Almighty to do wrong"* (Job 34:10). And James declares, *"God cannot be tempted by evil, nor does He tempt anyone"* (Jas. 1:13).

If sin doesn't come from the Devil, and it doesn't come from God, where does it come from? God tells us in Jeremiah 17:9 that *"the **heart** is deceitful above all things and beyond cure"* (emphasis mine). God also says, *"Each of you is following the stubbornness of his evil **heart** instead of obeying me"* (Jer. 16:12, emphasis mine). In other words, at the very core of our being is evil and deceit. Without Christ, it is part of who we are. Sin comes from within our own being. We are born sinners.

King David declared, *"Surely I was sinful at birth, sinful from the time my mother conceived me"* (Ps. 51:5). God Himself declares that *"every inclination of [man's] heart is evil from childhood"* (Gen. 8:21). It is part of our makeup to sin. Jesus said that it is *"from within, out of men's hearts, come evil thoughts"* (Mark 7:21).

Who Sins?
The third question we need to consider is this: Who sins? The answer is fairly obvious. We know that everyone sins! But the question and the answer are worth looking at in the light of God's Word. Galatians 3:22 tells us that *"the whole world is a prisoner of sin."* In Ecclesiastes 7:20 we read, *"There is not a righteous man on earth who does what is right and never sins."* You're probably familiar with Romans 3:23 where Paul writes, *"For all have sinned and fall short of the glory of God."* No, the devil did not make any of us do it. It is within our nature to sin.

You may think you're doing ok. And you may be convinced that you're not as bad as someone else. The Bible clearly teaches that *"there is no one who does not sin"* (1 Kings 8:46; 2 Chron. 6:36). God's Word asks the question, *"Who can say, 'I have kept my heart pure; I am clean and without sin'?"* (Prov. 20:9). The answer is no one. Even the greatest, most "holy" thing you may do is like a filthy rag before God (Isa.64:6).

"As it is written: 'There is no one righteous, not even one; there is no one who understands, no one who seeks God'" (Rom. 3:10-11). Who sins? Raise your hand high, my friend, right along with me, because we all sin.

Why Do I Sin?

Here is our fourth question to consider: Why do we give in to sin? The answer can be found in Hebrews 11:25 where we read that sin has its pleasures for a season. We give in to sin simply because we enjoy it! Let's face it, sin is pleasurable, as well as easy, effortless, and even comfortable. For example, it can feel good to explode in anger. Two people have an adulterous relationship because it feels good. A person may gossip or backbite to feel better about himself... or herself. Sin, indeed, does have its pleasures.

We need to pause for a moment to reflect on the fact that sin is pleasurable only "for a season." A season definitely refers to a period of time. That explosion of anger may have felt good, but the feeling of satisfaction is short-lived when compared to the devastation left in its wake. Adultery has its moment of physical elation, but it fades quickly, leaving long-lasting ramifications.

A season of pleasure also indicates something else. Having grown up in Indiana I have become quite familiar with the definition of "season." We experience all four of them in very succinct ways. You don't have to live here long, however, before you realize there is yet *another* type of season that we see all around us in Northern Indiana — corn! It's actually quite exciting to watch the farmers plow their fields, churning up all that fresh dark soil, and then plant the seed. As the corn season progresses through the warm summer months, we are able to almost literally watch the corn grow (I've even been told that on a quiet summers' eve you can actually *hear* the corn grow). What I have observed and learned is that every year the corn has a time of beginning and a time of harvest — a season.

God says that sin has its pleasure "for a season." Sin will grow. Sin can be quite pleasurable. But it lasts for only a season — for only a short period of time — at the end of which there *will* be a harvest. James says that *"sin, when it is full-grown, gives birth to death"* (Jas. 1:15). Job 4:8 tells us that *"those who plow evil and those who sow trouble reap it."* In Proverbs 22:8 we read, *"He who sows wickedness reaps trouble"* (NIV). You may be familiar with these words in Galatians 6:7-8 which say, *"Be not deceived; God is not mocked: for whatsoever a man soweth, that shall he also reap. For he that soweth to his flesh shall of the flesh reap corruption; but he that soweth to the Spirit shall of the Spirit reap life everlasting"* (KJV). Choose to sin and you will reap the effects. Choose to walk in the Spirit and reap the rewards.

*"I do not understand what I do. For what I want to do
I do not do, but what I hate I do"*
Romans 7:15

~ Five ~
Why Do We Sin? A Deeper Look

Ok. You give in to sin because the flesh likes it. The more you listen to the cries of your sinful flesh, the more you are going to sin. I remember being taught as a child the old adage, "What you feed, grows!" It's just like scratching a mosquito bite. The more you scratch, the more it itches. The more you scratch, the bigger it gets. The more you scratch, the more irritated it becomes and eventually turns into an open, festering wound. The more you sin, the more your flesh wants that forbidden pleasure and the larger the problem becomes. The solution to not irritating that mosquito bite is to stop scratching.

I'm going to ask you a very pointed question. In fact, I'm going to ask you to write your answer on a piece of paper or a blank page at the back of this book. There is great value in writing your answer down, as you will soon see. Here is the question: What are the sins you tend to battle against *daily*?

If you're like me, you probably put your pen down and are thinking to yourself, "I'm not going to write those things down for anyone else to see!" Pick the pen back up and write down the sins you tend to battle against daily. Be honest because we need our lists to stare us in the face. We need to take a moment to physically see on paper the names of the sins we tend to struggle with.

Look at your list. Now, look again. In each case, your mind plays an integral role in whether you will experience victory or defeat. In Romans 7:14-25 Paul says,

> *"We know that the law is spiritual; but I am unspiritual, sold as a slave to sin. I do not understand what I do. For what I want to do I do not do, but what I hate I do. And if I do what I do not want to do, I agree that the law is good. As it is, it is no longer I myself who do it, but it is sin living in me. I know that nothing good lives in me, that is, in my sinful nature. For I have the desire to do what is good, but I cannot carry it out. For what I do is not do the good I want to do; no, the evil I do not want to do — this I keep on doing. Now if I do what I do not want to do, it is no longer I who do it, but it is sin living in me that does it.*

> *"So I find this law at work: when I want to do good, evil is right there with me. For in my inner being I delight in God's law; but I see another law at work in the members of my body, waging war against the law of my mind and making me a prisoner of the law of sin at work within my members. What a wretched man I am! Who will rescue me from this body of death? Thanks be to God — through Jesus Christ our Lord! So then, I myself in my mind am a slave to God's law, but in my sinful nature a slave to the law of sin."*

I know that this passage can be confusing. To help us understand it a little better we are going to take the time to consider what Paul is saying. Look again at verse 15. *"I do not understand what I do. For what I want to do I do not do, but what I hate I do."* Can you relate? All too often I have struggled with doing the things I don't want to do while I don't do the things I want to. This is very frustrating, to say the least.

When I first began studying this entire passage in depth, I discovered that what was tripping me up were all the "I's" that Paul kept using. Let me share with you what I learned.

I Was Born A Sinner

As we move forward, you will see two diagrams that will help us understand and apply this wonderful text. First, I would like to introduce you to my friend Sy (see figure 3). Sy is a picture of what you and I were like before salvation.

Sy N. Ner
(fig.3)

As you take a look at Sy there are two things I want you to notice about him. First, notice that he has a sinful body. The second thing you should notice about my friend Sy is that, as an unsaved person, he also has an "old nature" residing within him (identified by the "ON" in the diagram). This is the picture of every human being ever born. Our old sinful nature, has a *natural* bent toward sin. Paul tells us in Ephesians 2:1-3 that this old nature has no desire or devotion for God in any way, shape, or form because it is dead in sin. It is focused entirely on one thing: gratifying the sinful cravings of the flesh. Anything the flesh wants, the old nature is willing to provide.

Notice that Paul says before salvation your *thoughts* were focused on gratifying the desires of the flesh (Eph. 2:3). Remember, what you think becomes what you do. Since the mind did not have anything holy and godly to help direct its thinking, it focused solely on fulfilling the pleasures of sin. Since the mind was bent toward fulfilling the requirements of the flesh for pleasure, the body gladly did whatever the mind wanted.

However, when you placed your faith in Jesus Christ as your Savior, something very interesting happened. Look carefully at what Paul says in Galatians 2:20, *"I have been crucified with Christ and I no longer live, but Christ lives in me. The life I live in the body, I live by faith in the Son of God, who loved me and gave himself for me."*

At the moment of salvation you were identified with Christ's death on the cross. But look again at this verse. Paul says, "I no longer live." Here he goes with the "I's" again. Who no longer lives? Paul? Is he referring to his physical life? Obviously not, since he's very much alive when writing this verse. So then, who or what was crucified? We need to focus very carefully on this because identifying the "I" in this verse is going to open up our understanding of Romans, chapter 7.

To identify the "I," think with me about the word "crucified." To be crucified meant to be put to death. The one who was crucified no longer had life — he was dead. The word "dead" means gone, never to come back to life — ever. Paul says, "I have been crucified." I have been put to death. The "I" Paul refers to — crucified, dead and gone, never to come back — is the old nature! The old nature that is focused on sin and self was crucified with Christ. The old nature that routinely led you into sin is dead. It's gone! It can never come back to life — ever! You no longer have an old nature. It died the day you were saved. Dead, gone, and never to come back again.

It is important to understand that when you put your faith in Christ, something very significant happened to your old nature. It is not hiding somewhere just waiting for the opportune time to raise its ugly head and pounce on you. Satan wants nothing more than to deceive God's children into believing that they should live in fear of that nasty old nature. He would like us to believe we're haunted by the ghost of the old nature, but fear no more my friend, because there are no such things as ghosts.

Paul writes, *"Therefore, if anyone is in Christ, he is a new creation; the old has gone, the new has come"* (2 Cor. 5:17). Wait a minute, "the old has gone"? — the old what? The word "old" in this verse refers to that which was from the beginning, that which you had since you were born. It is referring to that old sinful nature you used to have. Here is something exciting about the word "old": it refers not to chronological age but to that which is completely worn out and useless. That old sinful nature is gone and a new holy nature has come to take its place. Furthermore, that word "gone" means passed away, ceased to exist, no longer around. Your old nature is not here, nor will it ever come back; because it is crucified, dead — gone!

Ok, so the old sinful nature is dead and gone, never to come back to haunt you. Paul goes on to say in Galatians 2:20 that *"the life I live in the body, I live by faith."* Who is the "I" he is referring to now? We know it can't be the old nature because the old nature is dead and gone; it cannot come back to life. The "I" that Paul is referring to is the new nature that Christ has given us!

I am Born Again

Remember Paul's declaration in 2 Corinthians 5:17 that *"if anyone is in Christ, he is a new creation: the old has gone, the new has come!"* That word "new" doesn't mean refurbished. God didn't take your old nature and give it an overhaul. If He did, there would still be remnants of that old nature within you. No, He crucified the old sinful nature and put a brand-spanking-new holy nature within you. The word "new" in this verse carries with it the idea that it is of a totally different kind — not like the previous one at all. The old has gone and the new is here. Isn't that exciting! Paul also writes that the new self is *"created to be like God in true righteousness and holiness"* (Eph. 4:24). God is holy. So is your new nature.

The Almighty and Holy God has personally come to live inside of you! In order to dwell within us, He had to remove the old sinful nature and put a new nature in its place. A nature that is incapable of sinning. You see, if your nature could sin then God could not live there (Ps. 5:4-5; 101:7; Hab. 1:13). He created a completely different nature and placed it within you so that He could come in and make residence there! Now it's time to introduce you to another friend of mine who can help answer a few of our remaining questions. I would like you to meet Chris (see figure 4). Chris has a "new nature" (identified by the "NN" in the diagram).

Chris T. Yan (fig.4)

As you look at Chris you'll notice something similar to Sy. Chris also has a sinful body. You see, even though you are born-again, you still reside in a sinful body. Paul says that *"if Christ is in you, your body is dead because of sin, yet your spirit is alive because of righteousness"* (Rom. 8:10). In Romans 7:18 Paul says, *"I know that nothing good lives in me, that is, in my sinful nature."* The Greek word Paul uses for "sinful nature" is *sarx*, which is literally translated "flesh" and refers to the body in all of its humanness. What Paul is, in fact, saying in verse 18 is that nothing good lives in his flesh — his body — because it is sinful.

Before you accepted Christ as your Savior, both your body and spirit were dead. Now that you are saved, your spirit is alive in Christ, while your body is still dead in sin. No matter where you may be in your spiritual walk, your flesh is still dead in sin. Someday soon you will possess a resurrected, glorious body (Rom. 8:23; Phil. 3:21), but until then your body is just a lowly, sinful tent you are dwelling in (2 Cor. 4:7; 5:1). And because sin remains in your body, it is dead.

Now someone may ask about the passage of Scripture where Paul says, *"For we know that our old self was crucified with Him so that the body ruled by sin might be done away with, that we should no longer be slaves to sin"* (Rom. 6:6). Let me quickly point out that, yet again, we see the Biblical declaration that our old nature is dead and gone — crucified — never to come back. I love the fact that Paul uses the word *palaios* here for "old." *Palaios* refers to something that is completely worn out and useless, meant for the scrap heap. What an apt description of the old nature.

Notice that Paul declares that your old self was crucified with Jesus so that *the body ruled by sin* might be done away with. It's important that we understand the "body" Paul refers to here is not your physical body. It is a word that indicates a collective group of something (e.g., a student *body* is a collective group of students). The King James Version renders it "body of sin" and refers to the whole of sin. In other words, all of sin that has ruled over you is now done away with.

Simply put, Paul is talking about the influence that sin had over you. Do you see what has happened to that sinful influence? It has been "done away with." God has caused it to cease to have authority over you. With your old nature dead, sin no longer has power over you. That should make you want to jump up and down and shout! Because your old nature is dead and gone, you don't have to sin anymore. Glory!

My New Nature

John writes, *"No one who is born of God will continue to sin, because God's seed remains in him; he cannot go on sinning, because he has been born of God."* (1 John 3:9). To be honest, I struggled with this verse for a while. For quite a few years I battled with what Hebrews 12:1 calls a *"sin that so easily entangles."* It was a sin that I allowed to have control over me. It was a sin that nearly destroyed me, as well as my family. More than once I had a well-meaning Christian use 1 John 3:9 to tell me that since I continued to struggle with this particular sin, since it was a habitual act, I must not be saved. "After all," they would argue, "it says that no one who is born of God *will continue* to sin." Talk about discouraging!

Now I agree that on the surface it would appear the Bible is saying that if you habitually sin you are not a Christian. But I submit to you, that is not the message God is presenting here. As we look at this verse carefully there are a few things that are worthy of noting. The best way to make sense of all this is to break this text down into its smaller parts, examine those parts, and then put them back together again to look at the whole. We need to meditate on God's Word.

The first thing I want you to notice is that the phrase, "is born of God," is written in the perfect tense. Having been completed in the past, being born of God never needs to be repeated, ever again. What a great statement of eternal security. By using the perfect tense, John is saying that if you are born of God, you are saved now and forever. It doesn't matter what sins you have committed or ever will commit, Christ died on the cross for all of them. Not a single sin has ever taken, or ever will take God by surprise making Him say, "Oh, I didn't know you were going to do that. I'm sorry, but your salvation is nullified." Praise the Lord our salvation is entirely dependent upon an Omniscient and Sovereign God and not our own efforts! It's not by works of righteousness that you have done but according to His mercy that He saved you (Titus 3:5).

We also need to note that the phrase, "is born of God," is written in the passive voice, which means it is being done to you or for you, not by you. In other words, you cannot save yourself. God did it entirely for you. *"For it is by grace you have been saved, through faith — and this not from yourselves, it is the gift of God — not by works, so that no one can boast"* (Eph. 2:8-9). In talking about the Christian, John has established that the believer is *born of God*, once and for all, He accomplished it by His powerful will, and thus you cannot lose your salvation.

Next, notice that John says, *"no one…will continue"* (1 John 3:9). Here is where many have stumbled into murky waters because they did not carefully examine what is being said. Look at this verse as it is rendered in the King James Version:

"Whosoever is born of God doth not commit sin; for His seed remaineth in him; and he cannot sin, because he is born of God." Notice the word "not" (doth *not* commit sin). This is a term in the Greek that expresses a full and direct negation. In other words, absolutely not ever! John is saying that whoever is born of God does not *ever* commit sin. Now stay with me on this. John writes this in the indicative mood, which means that this is a simple statement of fact, period. In other words, it is a simple statement of fact that that which is born of God *will not ever* sin! There is nothing here about habitual sins. Nothing to indicate that as long as you're not repeatedly sinning you're spiritually safe. That which is born of God never sins — ever!

Please don't brand me a heretic and slam this book shut in disgust never to pick it up again, at least not yet. Hear me out. Have you ever put your faith and trust in Jesus Christ as your Lord and Savior? If so, you are a born-again Christian. Now let me ask you this: Have you committed the same sin more than once since becoming a Christian? More than even two or three times? I am going to assume your answer is "yes" (Eccles. 7:20; 1 John 1:8; 2:1). So does this verse say that since you have committed the same sin more than once you are no longer a Christian, or that you never were? Of course not! What, then, is it saying?

To help answer this question, we need to identify exactly what it is that is *born of God*. Our key to understanding this is in the second half of the verse. John goes on to explain how that which is born of God does not sin because God's *seed* remains in the Christian; and he (that is, the seed) cannot sin, because he (the seed) has been born of God. Focus your attention on that little word "seed." It is the Greek word *sperma* and refers to an offspring; that which was created by God.

What did God create that is now within you? Paul wrote, *"If anyone is in Christ, he is a **new creation**; the old has gone, the new has come"* (2 Cor. 5:17, emphasis mine). The new *what* has come? The new nature that every Christian received at the moment of salvation is *what* has come. Remember what Paul said in Galatians 2:20, *"I no longer live, but Christ lives in me."* That "seed" John refers to is the new nature that God created and placed within you, and it "remains," it continues to abide or dwell — to live — within you.

Now look at what John says about that new nature. He states that the one born of God will not commit sin "because" God's seed (the new nature) remains in him. That word "because" points to something that rests upon a patent fact. John is declaring it to be a patent fact that the reason that which is born of God (the new nature) will not ever sin is because it is God's seed, His perfect creation, which is abiding within the believer.

John goes on to say that God's seed *"cannot go on sinning."* The word "cannot" is the Greek word *dunamai* and refers to an absence of power or ability. In other words, that which is born of God does not have the power or ability to accomplish the task of sinning. If you are a Christian, then God says you have a new nature within you. That new nature (God's seed) cannot sin because it is born of God and has God's nature — a holy nature which is incapable of sinning because it doesn't have the power to do so!

This is a crucial point we must not forget as it plays a very important role in the rest of this book. Let me reiterate that the moment you were saved your old nature was crucified; it is dead and gone. In its place God created a new nature, one that is holy and incapable of sinning. That new, holy nature is alive within you, dear Christian. It is your true identity, don't ever forget that!

Look again at Romans 6:6. *"For we know that our old self was crucified with Him so that the body of sin might be done away with, that we should **no longer be slaves to sin**"* (emphasis mine). According to this text you are no longer a slave to sin, because sin no longer has power over you. Colossians 3:3 says, *"For you died, and your life is now hidden with Christ in God."* Notice the words, "for you died." This is a phrase that refers to that which is consummated and finished. In other words, it is totally and completely dead. At the moment of your salvation that old nature died. You are now alive in Christ!

Lest we lose sight of the purpose of this book, look at what Paul is emphasizing in Colossians 3:1-2. *"Since, then, you have been raised with Christ, set your hearts on things above, where Christ is seated at the right hand of God. Set your minds on things above, not on earthly things."* The point I want to make here is not that we are alive in Christ, although that, in and of itself, is amazing. Rather, because the old nature is dead, because we are alive in Christ, we must firmly plant our hearts and our minds on things above, not on earthly things. What you think becomes what you do, so if you are going to bring glory to God in your daily life, He must first be glorified in your thought life, as you submit to the power of Christ now living in you.

The Ugh in Struggle

Someone may respond, "Steve, I now understand that I have a new nature that is incapable of sinning and that sounds great, but I still struggle with sin every day!" I'm right there with you my friend. I agree wholeheartedly because I too struggle with sin every day. In fact, that is exactly what Paul is talking about in Romans 7:15-25. The exciting thing here is that our struggle is not because we still have an old sinful nature plaguing us, dogging every step of our spiritual walk. As we've learned, that nature is dead and forever gone. We struggle for an entirely different reason.

Consider this: the 'I' that is struggling with sin *is* your new nature. The entire reason you struggle with sin is because you have a new, holy nature within you that is in constant battle with the sinful tendencies of the flesh. Galatians 5:17 says, *"For the sinful nature (flesh) desires what is contrary to the Spirit, and the Spirit what is contrary to the sinful nature (flesh). They are in conflict with each other, so that you do not do what you want."* This is why you still struggle with sin. Only the new nature is going to find

47

sin appalling. Only the new nature is going to see sin as an enemy that must be defeated. It is only in the life of a born again believer that the new nature will fight against the flesh, because it is only within believers that the Holy Spirit dwells. The flesh sets itself against the work that God is doing in your life through your new nature.

An unsaved person may regret a sinful thing they have done, and may even experience guilt and the consequences of their sinful actions, but they are not experiencing spiritual warfare — whereas a Christian does. Until the day comes when you are called home to heaven to spend eternity with God, you will exist here on earth as a redeemed child of God living in an unredeemed body — the perfect combination, ripe for conflict. Living a life that glorifies God is not simply a matter of passive surrender ("Let go, and let God"). It is a life filled with conflict because our new nature is in constant combat with the sinful desires of the flesh (Gal. 5:17). This is why Paul says, *"We wait eagerly for...the redemption of our bodies"* (Rom. 8:23). There is coming a time when Jesus Christ "shall transform our lowly bodies so that they will be like His glorious body" (Phil. 3:21). Until that day, dear Christian friend, you and I are going to struggle with sin.

Consider again what Paul wrote in Romans 7:21-25:

> *"So I find this law at work: Although I want to do good, evil is right there with me. For in my inner being I delight in God's law; but I see another law at work in me, waging war against the law of my **mind** and making me a prisoner of the law of sin at work within me. What a wretched man I am! Who will rescue me from this body that is subject to death? Thanks be to God, who delivers me through Jesus Christ our Lord! So then, I myself in my **mind** am a slave to God's law, but in my sinful nature a slave to the law of sin" (emphasis mine).*

When the new nature wants to do what is good — to bring glory to God by yielding to His will — evil is right there with

48

you. You live in a body that is prone to sin. Paul says that in your inner being, that is, in your new nature, you delight in God's law. But your body finds pleasure in sin. The result is an all-out conflict — an ongoing conflict where the battlefield *is* the mind (Rom. 7:23). It is no wonder that Paul said he was a wretched man. It is no wonder that Paul glorifies God for his deliverance through Jesus!

"When tempted, no one should say, 'God is tempting me.'
For God cannot be tempted by evil, nor does
He tempt anyone"
James 1:13

~ Six ~
A Look at Temptation

Everyone struggles with temptation; it's a fact of life. Whether it's fighting the urge to eat that second piece of cake, fudge a little on your tax return, lie to your spouse about where you were and what you were doing, steal a lustful glance at that girl on the beach, or not tell your boss the whole story, temptation to sin is all around us.

Usually, along with the temptation comes the desire to blame someone or something else. "Well, if my boss weren't so demanding...," "If my wife would give me a little more leeway...," "If she didn't dress so provocatively...," we argue. Our tendency is to feel that we have no option, that God has somehow put us in this situation.

In the book of James, we read:

> *"When tempted, no one should say, 'God is tempting me.' For God cannot be tempted by evil, nor does He tempt anyone; but each one is tempted when, by his own evil desire, he is dragged away and enticed. Then, after desire has conceived, it gives birth to sin; and sin, when it is full-grown, gives birth to death" (Jas. 1:13-15).*

We need to park here for a few minutes and consider what God is telling us. First, look again at verse 14 and think with me about the words "dragged away." When you think of someone being dragged away, what comes to mind? It almost gives the idea that you're being kidnapped — taken kicking and screaming, against your will. But that is *not* what this phrase means here. This is not something that happens to you unawares and against your will.

No Fishing Allowed

It is a fishing term that is literally translated "drawn away," and refers to being lured away from a place of safety. It's been a long time since I've gone fishing, but if I remember correctly, the purpose of the lure is to disguise the deadly hook by providing an enticement to the fish. What would happen if a fisherman simply tossed a bare hook into the water without the lure? Absolutely nothing.

The lure — usually a big, juicy, squirming earthworm — is placed into the water and the unsuspecting fish, swimming merrily on its way, catches a glimpse of something attractive out of the corner of its eye. Intrigued, it changes the direction it was swimming to go check it out. Cautiously at first, it begins to play with the lure. Finally, convinced that it poses no threat and is quite appealing, it sucks in the lure and speeds off, thereby embedding the deadly hook into its mouth. The lure has done its job! The result is death.

So what is the lure that draws us away? The answer is found in James 1:14. We are lured; we are drawn away by *"our own evil desires."* In other words, there is a particular lust or a craving you have for sinful pleasure and you allow yourself to *think about* how to satisfy it. It begins as a tickle in the back of your mind. Your thought process considers it, weighing out the pros and cons, the risks vs. the pleasure it promises. Then, as that thought becomes stronger, it creates within you a desire to put that thought into action. Like the fish, you cautiously play around with it for a while. When nothing bad happens, you selfishly suck it in and try to speed off without getting caught. When you do, wham!

Why do we even fool around with it? Why do we even allow our minds to think about it, letting it divert our attention away from God? Again, the answer is in verse 14 — it "entices" you. It appeals to your sinful, fleshly desires for ease and pleasure, and brings a type of excitement and arousal, even comfort. You think about it. Thinking about it feels good. Thinking about it increases the anticipation and the desire for fleshly comfort and pleasure. You let your mind dwell on it until eventually you act upon those thoughts. Remember: what we think becomes what we do.

You see, when you entertain wrong thoughts, those thoughts will eventually produce wrong actions. For example, if you allow your mind to dwell on improper sexual thoughts you will eventually act upon those thoughts. You might go to the Internet and visit adult-oriented websites. You might look upon someone of the opposite sex in an improper way. You may develop unrealistic expectations in your marriage. You may seek out an extra-marital relationship. You might even commit a crime all in the name of sexual lust.

Or perhaps your husband isn't carrying his load around the house. He comes home from work and just crashes on the couch with paper in hand. He expects you to get dinner ready for him while you keep the kids out of his hair. Your thoughts turn to how unfair it is and how inconsiderate he is. You believe you deserve better. You begin to feel a sense of discontentment, which leads to anger and bitterness. The result is a death to your relationship. Entertaining wrong thoughts will lead to wrong behavior.

If you entertain prideful thoughts your actions will eventually be self-focused, self-purposed — geared to draw attention to "King Me" for the sole purpose of pleasing only self, usually at the expense of others. If you entertain thoughts of fear, anger, anxiety, bitterness (on the list goes), your actions will fall into step accordingly. Conversely, if you focus on thoughts of glorifying God what will happen? You will end up giving God the glory in all that you say and do! James is telling us that we sin because we see the lure of some type of sinful pleasure, it entices us, we think about it, and the result is that we commit a sinful act, which in turn leads to death.

One of Satan's major battle-tactics is that of keeping the Christian thinking they are defeated, still in bondage to sin. When he accomplishes this, he has succeeded in diminishing our potential for the kingdom of God. If he can get you to feel defeated in your sin, to believe that you're never going to change — after all, you're only human and you still have that sinful nature — then you will eventually give up trying. You will learn to accept that sinful aspect of your life and eventually even embrace it.

Anytime you choose to not deal with a sin issue in your life, it will ultimately lead to a hardened heart. A hard heart happens when you hear God's truth, believe what He says is indeed truth, yet repeatedly choose to do nothing about it. Every time you do this, your heart hardens ever so slightly. The temptation becomes stronger and you fight it less. The sin has a stronger hold in your life and the conviction you feel over that sin loses its grip. Every time you recognize a sin in your life, feel the convicting power of the Holy Spirit, and yet do nothing about it, you become less sensitive — your conscience is being *"seared as with a hot iron"* (1 Tim. 4:2). Over time, you will become callous to the promptings of the Holy Spirit and suppress His fire (1 Thess. 5:19); just like closing the door on a lantern, no longer allows the light to shine for others to see.

I want to encourage you that there is hope! Paul writes in Philippians 1:6 that he is *"confident of this, that He who began a good work in you will carry it on to completion until the day of Christ."* You see, *"It is God who works in you to will and to act according to His good purpose"* (Phil. 2:13). God has a plan for your life (Jer. 29:11). He is not going to allow sin to thwart His purpose. He will never leave you to the wolves. Don't allow yourself to get bogged down in trying to figure out *how* to have victory over sin in your life. Focus your attention on growing in your relationship with God, who is able to strengthen you to do all things (Phil. 4:13), and victory will follow!

One Plus One Equals What?

The sin you give in to is not the only sin you will struggle with. One sin inevitably leads to another, and then to another. Once you become comfortable with a sin in your life, it is only a matter of time until other issues arise. For example, the husband who has been secretly looking at pornography on his computer isn't only dealing with the sin of lust. By keeping it secret, he is guilty of deceit and lying as well. If his wife suspects something and confronts him, he may choose to lie about it, possibly responding in anger. If the sin continues, his battle with such sins as pride, anger, and bitterness will deepen.

Sin will *always* result in death. Think about it this way, if left to itself, the process will always be temptation ==> sin ==> death (Jas. 1:15). Whenever you sin, there is always a death that follows. Again, let's use the husband entrenched in pornography as an example. He is battling with sin on a number of different fronts (lust, pride, anger, controlling fear, etc.). As a result, his sin has brought death to his relationship with his wife. She may not even know it (although my experience has shown that a wife usually suspects it). The marriage relationship has begun to deteriorate. He becomes withdrawn, self-focused, and self-obsessed. He no longer reaches out to her, caring for her, and loving her the way he used to. Their physical relationship has also begun to die. This in turn causes *her* to withdraw, eventually destroying her love for him — another death. Sin will always result in some kind of death, something is always destroyed.

Too often we listen to the lies of the enemy: "I'm just human, nobody is perfect. I am always going to struggle with sin anyway, so why fight it?" My friend, all believers, including you, have the ability to say no to temptation. God is not a liar (Titus 1:2; Heb. 6:18; 1 John 2:21). God — who cannot lie — tells us that we can do all things through Jesus, because in Him we'll find the strength to accomplish it (Phil. 4:13). God — who cannot lie — promises us that *"no temptation has seized you except what is common to man. And God is faithful; He will not let you be tempted beyond what you can bear. But when you are tempted, He will also provide a way out so that you can stand up under it"* (1 Cor. 10:13). So don't you ever, *ever* let the lie of the enemy convince you that you cannot have victory in the face of temptation, especially over the temptations that so easily entangle you (Heb. 12:1), because God says otherwise. God is truth and no lie ever comes from the truth (1 John 2:21).

Unique You're Not

There is no, "But Steve, you don't understand." There is no, "But my situation is different." Look at 1 Corinthians 10:13 again: *"No temptation has seized you except what is common to man..."* Think about that. Paul uses the word "no" which is an absolute negative. In other words, absolutely not a single temptation will ever come upon you that is totally unique to you. Not one. We all struggle with temptation. Every Christian battles every day with sin issues in their life. Paul said it is *common* to man. We all experience the same temptation. It may have a different face and be experienced in a different way, but it's still the same temptation. It's a war, my friend (Rom. 7:23; Eph. 6:10-17). You will always be tempted; it's part of the Christian life. But you never have to give in to the temptation. You never *have* to sin. Others have experienced the same temptation and have been victorious over it. So can you!

God understands the apparent dominance that sin presents. It seems like it is going to overwhelm you and you are getting swept away in its powerful flow. Paul says that no temptation has *seized* you. "Seized" is a word that means to grab hold of and carry away. God's promise to every Christian is that no temptation, even though it feels like it has dug its nasty claws deep into you, no temptation will be so strong that you cannot stand with Christ in the face of it. Again let me remind you that

Paul said "no temptation," not a single one ever has been, nor ever will be, stronger than God.

I love it when I see the words "but God" in Scripture (look at 1 Cor. 10:13 in the KJV). No temptation, even the one that gives you the feeling of powerlessness, is stronger than God. *"But God is faithful,"* my friend. That word "faithful" refers to one who has been repeatedly proven trustworthy in the execution of their promise and the discharge of their official duty. The one who is faithful can be fully and completely relied upon to keep their word and do exactly what they have promised. Who is faithful, fully trustworthy, and completely reliable to keep their every word and promise? Who will, with the temptation, help you to endure? The answer is: God, the Almighty, Holy, all-powerful, sovereign Creator of the universe!

God is faithful. He knows about your temptation and He has promised that He will give you the ability to endure. He doesn't want you to be defeated or discouraged. He doesn't want you to feel the only choice is to sin. God will not let you be tempted beyond what you can bear. This of course does not mean that you will never experience a temptation. Nor does it mean that the temptations you do experience won't seem overwhelming at times. It does, however, mean that God is in control, even when you are being tempted. In the midst of that temptation, you can fully trust in God that He will not permit that temptation to be more than you can deal with.

Let me be quick to point out — to remind you — that God is not the one who tempts you to sin (Jas. 1:13). God allows the temptations to enter your life for the purpose of revealing to you a sin issue that is preventing you from growing closer to Him. If Satan had his way, that temptation would bring about your destruction. But God uses it as a way to show you that there is an area of weakness in your life that needs to be dealt with so that you can have a more intimate relationship with Him. Through that temptation God is providing you with an opportunity to discover what sin issues you are still struggling with. And in the midst of that temptation, He shows you how to escape — how to stand in truth.

Paul uses the words "can bear" in the present tense, active voice, and indicative mood. If you recall, present tense refers to the immediate here and now, in real time. Active voice means you are the one doing the action — in this case, enduring the temptation. Indicative mood means it is a simple statement of fact. In other words, it is a simple fact that as you personally, right this very moment, are going through a temptation, no matter how overwhelming it may seem, you have the resources and ability to endure it. God makes sure of that.

The key is how you deal with your temptation *when* it comes. Note that temptation *will* come. Paul says, *"**when** you are tempted,"* not *if* you are tempted. James tells us to *"consider it pure joy…whenever you face trials of many kinds"* (Jas. 1:2, emphasis mine). We will always struggle with temptation. The key is how you handle it. And how you manage it begins with your mind — what you allow yourself to think about in the midst of the temptation. If you look at the temptation with a defeatist attitude, you will end up being defeated. However, if you see the temptation as God revealing something in your life that needs to be dealt with so that you can mature and conform to the image of Christ, then you will take a totally different approach to the temptation. This is the way you are able to endure it.

"God is faithful; He will not let you be tempted beyond what you can bear. But when you are tempted, He will also provide a way out so that you can stand up under it" (1 Cor. 10:13). The way out that God provides is not that you will no longer experience the temptation. That "way out" would not help you grow closer to Him. That way would not help you become more like Christ. That kind of "way out" gives you the opportunity to slip back into your contented way of living. It makes it easy for you, and God isn't about making life easy. Rather, as you are going through the temptation, you are to focus your mind on the

things of God, focus your attention on what it is that God is revealing to you and what you need to do to deal with it.

As God shows you from His Word, you then apply it to your life. Ask yourself these three questions: What is this verse really saying? How does this apply to me? What do I need to do in my life as a result of the truths contained here? This is your way of escape. Not that you will no longer face this temptation, but that it will no longer feel overbearing and overpowering. You will be able to endure — bear up under the temptation patiently — because now you know how to handle it victoriously.

Getting a Fix

The key to dealing with temptation and experiencing victory over sin begins with what goes on in your mind — how you think. What is your mind focused upon in the midst of the temptation? God's command is clear, you are to *"set your minds on things above, not on earthly things"* (Col. 3:2). The verb that Paul uses, "to set," involves making something firm and immovable — fixed or planted — almost as if it were set into cement. Now, according to Colossians 3:2, your *mind* is to be firmly, immovably planted on something. It is not to wander away from that upon which it is set, no matter what enticing lure may come your way. A set mind is an immovable mind. A set mind is fixed and focused on one thing. As Paul says, that something is the "things above." You and I must make our minds firmly and immovably planted on things above.

The next question we need to focus on is this: What are the "things above" that we should be thinking about? It is interesting that Paul uses the definite article here. I know it doesn't read well, but by using the article in the sentence, we can see what Paul is actually saying: "Set your minds on things THE above." By writing it that way, he is making it clear that he's not referring to an ambiguous "above" that we can define however we want. If left to ourselves, the type of "things above" that we might we set our minds on would probably not be the things of God (Ps. 10:4).

59

By using the article, Paul helps us understand that there is one singular thing our minds are to be set upon — Heaven, God's throne! Our minds are to be firmly, immovably fixed on the things of God. Remember, what you think about directly affects what you say and what you do. And each and every thing you say and do should bring glory to God. *This* is why your mind must be firmly and immovably planted on God. If your mind is firmly planted on self, your words and deeds will be self-centered as well. When your mind is completely focused on God, all of your words and actions will be for His honor and glory.

Notice that Paul writes this verb, "set," in the present tense, active voice, and imperative mood. The present tense simply means that the action is being done now and never ends. It is continuous — on going, and always in the present. According to this verse, the action that is continuously being done is that our minds are being firmly and immovably planted on God.

However, this is not something that automatically happens for you or to you. The active voice means you are the one doing the action. You are the one who is setting your mind — firmly and immovably planting your thoughts — on God, not letting it wander. It is personal. No one else can do this for you, you must do it yourself or it won't get done.

Finally, the imperative mood is a command. This is something that is your responsibility as a child of God. You MUST fix your mind firmly on the things of God. If you don't, you are sinning. Our minds must not ever wander away from the goal of glorifying God in everything we think, say, and do.

Look carefully at this verse again, *"Set your minds on things above, not on earthly things"* (Col. 3:2). You are commanded (imperative mood) to firmly and immovably plant (set) your mind on God. You can't set my mind for me and I can't set yours for you — you have to do it yourself (active voice). Setting your mind on the things of God is not something you do just once in the morning and then go on with your day. You must do this continuously (present tense). Now that is powerful stuff!

In 1 Chronicles 22:19 we read, *"Set your heart and your soul to seek the Lord your God."* Are you firmly planting your mind — the very core of your being — on seeking God (1 Chron. 16:11; 28:9; cp. Matt. 6:33)? Think about this for a moment. If your mind were firmly and immovably planted on the things of God so that even the most tempting and enticing lure didn't draw you away, your life would be different. Your words and deeds would be different.

If you are going to glorify God in your daily life, you must first glorify Him in your thought life. But *how* do we do that? We *set* our mind on God. We make every thought we think a thought that brings glory to our Heavenly Father.

"Live by the Spirit, and you will not gratify the desires of the sinful nature"
Galatians 5:16-17

~ Seven ~
Living by the Spirit

As long as you live here on earth you're going to battle daily with your sinful flesh, there's just no way to get around it (Rom. 7:15-25). The great news is that although you will always struggle *against* the desires of the flesh, you do not have to be defeated by them. God promises that when you *"live by the Spirit, you will not gratify the desires of the sinful nature [flesh]"* (Gal. 5:16-17, addition mine).

Consider this carefully: to gain spiritual victory over the flesh, you need to live by the Spirit. Ok, that sounds great, and we know it's true because God said it; but what does that mean? How exactly does a Christian *live* by the Spirit?

First, let's make sure we understand what *living by the Spirit* means. The word "living" is defined as regulating or conducting your life according to a specific purpose and guide. It is a term that refers to taking charge of your life in such a way that you are making constant decisions and adjustments throughout the day to conduct yourself according to the leading of the Holy Spirit. And how does the Holy Spirit lead you? How do you know what the Spirit wants you to do? He uses God's truth — the Scriptures — to guide you (John 16:13). As you read God's Word, study it, memorize it, and meditate on it, the Holy Spirit will bring to your remembrance what God says you should do every time you face a decision. Just as God promised the Children of Israel in Isaiah 30:21, so His promise stands for us today: *"Whether you turn to the right or to the left, your ears will hear a voice behind you, saying, 'This is the way; walk in it.'"* The Holy Spirit is that voice, guiding you through the promises and principles of God's Word.

Paul wrote this phrase, "live by the Spirit," in the present tense, active voice, and imperative mood. By now you are somewhat familiar with these terms. Present tense refers to a continuous, ongoing, regular action that is happening in real time. It is something that you need to do every moment of every day. By using the present tense, Paul is telling us that every moment of every day you need to regulate your life; conducting yourself according to the leading of the Holy Spirit. As the Spirit reveals God's truth to you — showing you things you need to either do or stop doing — you immediately yield your life to Him and put that truth into action in your life. This is living by the Spirit in the present tense.

The active voice means that this is something that *you* have to do. No one else can do it for you. It is personal. If you don't do it, it won't get done. Living every moment of every day under the direction of the Holy Spirit is something that only you can do. Only you can hear the promptings of the Holy Spirit as He guides you into God's truth. Only you can make the decision to yield to His will and apply God's truth immediately to your life.

Finally, the imperative mood means this isn't an option — it's a command. We are commanded by God to conduct our everyday living according to the leading of the Holy Spirit. He commands it because He knows it is best for us.

Notice, as well, that the verb, "live by" (the King James Version renders it "walk by"), indicates forward movement. In other words, you are going from where you are right now to where you ought to be. We often call this "spiritual growth." Only as you submit your life to the Spirit's control will you move forward — growing spiritually. You see, step-by-step the Holy Spirit moves you from where you are to where God is leading you, where He wants you to be. The Holy Spirit is your guide. This is exactly why Paul said that when you live by the Spirit you will not gratify the sinful desires of the flesh.

The fact is, you cannot live the Christian life by your own strength and resources any more than you could save yourself for eternity (Gal. 3:1-3). The victorious Christian life is a life lived under the direction of, and through the power of, the Holy Spirit. The Spirit of God is not some force or power for you to use. He is a Person of the Godhead to whom you are to yield, and to *let Him use you*! I submit that holy living doesn't come from the things you do for God, but from what He does through you as you *live by* the Holy Spirit. God has placed His Spirit within you to be your guide.

Living by the Spirit is what Paul calls "transformation" in Romans 12:2. In Ephesians 3:16 Paul says, *"I pray that out of His glorious riches He may strengthen you with power through His Spirit in your inner being."* Think about that. God strengthens us with His unlimited power through the Spirit, His Spirit. It is through God's Spirit that we receive God's strength in our inner being — our new nature! Remember, when you live by the Spirit you will not gratify the desires of the flesh (Gal. 5:16).

Never forget the integral role your mind plays in living a life that glorifies God. Paul commands you to *"clothe yourselves with the Lord Jesus Christ, and do not think about how to gratify the desires of the [flesh]"* (Rom. 13:14, emphasis mine). Let me reiterate the point that if you are going to glorify God in your everyday living you must first glorify Him in your every-moment thinking. What you think becomes what you do. You are to put on godly behavior, but the only way that is going to be consistently characteristic of your life is if you radically change your thinking. You are to no longer think about how to gratify the desires of your flesh. Rather, focus your thoughts on how to glorify God. You are to live by the Spirit — regulate your life every moment of every day by submitting to the leading of the Holy Spirit. And in doing that, you are saying "no" to the constant cravings of your sinful flesh.

Mercy Me

In Romans 12:1 Paul writes, *"Therefore, I urge you, brothers, in view of God's mercy, to offer your bodies as living sacrifices, holy and pleasing to God — this is your spiritual act of worship."* Paul isn't saying here, "Wow. It would be great if you could offer your body daily to God. You really ought to think about doing that." No, he says, *"I urge you."* In other words, "I am calling you to my side to lovingly admonish you, to beseech you, to exhort you — this is of utmost importance — offer your bodies every moment to God as a living sacrifice." These words should cause us to sit up and take notice. Paul is exhorting us because of the mercy God has given us.

Paul is speaking with urgency because of an understanding of God's mercy. "Mercy" is a word that refers to compassion and pity. It has been said that His mercy is, "God not giving to us what we deserve." Think about that. *"He saved us, not because of righteous things we had done, but because of His mercy. He saved us through the washing of rebirth and renewal by the Holy Spirit"* (Titus 3:5). Peter said, *"In [God's] great mercy He has given us new birth into a living hope through the resurrection of Jesus Christ from the dead"* (1 Pet. 1:3). We deserve death, not life. Yet God, in His mercy has declared that anyone who believes on His Son will not receive the death they deserve, but will have eternal life (1 Tim. 1:16)!

God's mercy is great (2 Sam. 24:14; 1 Chron. 21:13), and He shows us His great mercy because of His great love (Neh. 13:22; Ps. 25:6; Eph. 2:4). It is because of God's mercy that He does not abandon us (Neh. 9:31), and that we are able to come boldly into His presence without fear (Ps. 5:7; Heb. 4:16). God has promised His mercy to those who reject sinful thinking, turn to the Lord, and confess and renounce their sin (Prov. 28:13; Isa. 55:7). In fact, God delights in showing us His mercy (Mic. 7:18).

So, *"in view of God's mercy,"* because of the fact that God has not given to you what you deserve, Paul urges you to offer your body to God. His call is for every believer to dedicate every aspect of themselves without reservation to the Lord. Let me emphasize the fact that this exhortation is given only to the born-again believer. Paul calls us "brothers." You see, *"The man without the Spirit does not accept the things that come from the Spirit of God, for they are foolishness to him, and he cannot understand them, because they are spiritually discerned"* (1 Cor. 2:14). Only the born-again believer can present their body as a living sacrifice to God, because only the Christian can come before God with such an offering. The unsaved haven't recognized their need, and accepted God's gift of washing and renewing by the Word and the Spirit. They are not presentable before God; therefore, they cannot serve or worship God in any way that will be acceptable to Him.

The Offering

Focus for a moment on the fact that you are to "offer" your body to God. The word "offer" is a technical term that was used to describe the way a priest places an offering on the altar with the intention of surrendering or yielding it up to God. Anytime something was placed on an altar, it was for the purpose of sacrifice — willingly putting it to death, giving ownership up. As a Christian, *"you also, like living stones, are being built into a spiritual house to be a **holy priesthood, offering spiritual sacrifices** acceptable to God through Jesus Christ"* (1 Pet. 2:5, emphasis mine). As a child of God you are considered a "priest," and, as such, you are to offer — to daily yield — your body to God. This is your priestly act of worship. You are called to make your body available for God to use — every moment of every day — in any way He desires.

Why present our bodies as a sacrifice to God? Think about it this way; imagine you are driving down the road in a vehicle that desperately needs its wheels aligned. You have to constantly fight with the steering wheel just to keep the car going straight. The moment you let go of the wheel, the vehicle naturally veers off to the right or to the left, placing you at high risk for an accident. This is much the same with your body. Left to itself, the natural bent of your body is to sin. To prevent that from happening, you have to daily grab hold of the "wheel" and fight with it to keep it going in the correct direction. You must daily — moment by moment — place your body on the altar, yielding it completely to the will of the Spirit to do service for God instead of serving self.

Your body is more than just the physical shell you see in the mirror every morning. It is also the place where your sinful humanness resides. In fact, your humanness is an integral part of your body — they are inseparable. If you allow it, your body can, and will, frustrate the desires of your new nature to please God. Your body is still the beachhead of sin. It is permanently out of alignment; and if left to its own, it will steer you wrong every time. As long as you are alive here on earth, your new nature will reside in a sinful body of flesh that can readily give in to sinful thoughts and longings. This is why you are to continually present your body to God as a living sacrifice.

The Bible exhorts you to *"not let sin reign in your mortal body so that you obey its evil desires"* (Rom. 6:12). I find it interesting that Paul uses the word "not," which is an absolute negation, in this verse. In other words, in no way or at any time is this to ever happen. Sin must never be allowed to reign in your body. A second interesting fact in this verse is that the words "let reign" refer to exercising kingly power over someone. If you do not submit control of your body to God's Spirit in your new nature, sin will walk all over you. Your flesh desires to be king, reigning over your new nature, and dictating what you will and will not do. If you allow sin to rule in your body, you will end up obeying it instead of God.

Think for a moment about the word "obey." To obey is to listen to the command of another and do what you have been told. When you obey your flesh, you are choosing to deny God's truth and ignore the promptings of the Holy Spirit, favoring the desires of your sinful nature.

The word Paul uses for "desires" refers to cravings and longings for *that which is forbidden* — the things you, as a child of God, should *not* do. Jesus said, *"No one can serve two masters. Either he will hate the one and love the other, or he will be devoted to the one and despise the other. You cannot serve both God and Money"* (Matt. 6:24; cp Luke 16:13). You are faced with a choice daily. God's command is that you make the choice to not let sin reign, otherwise you will end up obeying its evil desires and conversely disobeying God. The way you make that choice is to offer your body as a living sacrifice every day. Choose to yield to God moment by moment through His Spirit.

"Don't you know that when you offer yourselves to someone to obey him as slaves, you are slaves to the one whom you obey — whether you are slaves to sin, which leads to death, or to obedience, which leads to righteousness" (Rom. 6:16)? You make choices throughout each day that reveal who you are yielding to in obedience. Do you let sin reign so that you obey its desires, or do you say no to ungodliness, and choose to live by the Spirit in obedience to God? The bottom line is that *"those who obey His commands live in Him, and He in them. And this is how we know that He lives in us: We know it by the Spirit He gave us"* (1 John 3:24). Love for God is demonstrated when you *"obey His commands. And His commands are not burdensome"* (1 John 5:3), because God gave you His Spirit to direct you and give you strength to obey Him — to accomplish what He has commanded. The choice is yours.

Body Parts
The fact is you cannot live a godly life apart from your body. You are dependent upon your body for more than just living, breathing, and moving around in. It is through the use of your body that you either glorify God or magnify self. This is why it's so vital that you learn how to yield to the Spirit's control of your body, and so that you can offer it daily as a sacrifice to God.

We know that our aim as a Christian is to glorify God in everything we say and do. But consider this very carefully: you cannot glorify God in your daily life apart from your body. Peter says you are to *"live such good lives among the pagans that, though they accuse you of doing wrong, they may* **see your good deeds** *and glorify God"* (1 Pet. 2:12, emphasis mine). How can the unsaved see your good deeds apart from your body? They can't. Jesus admonishes you to *"let your light shine before men, that they may* **see your good deeds** *and praise your Father in heaven"* (Matt. 5:16, emphasis mine). The activities you choose to do with your body are what people see. Are the attitudes and actions you choose going to bring glory to God or attention to self? It is when you yield to God through His Spirit in your daily actions, that you bear much fruit and show yourself to be His disciple (John 15:8).

The bottom line is this: when you choose to let the flesh rule in your life, your attitudes and actions will reveal it, because *"The acts of the (flesh) are obvious: sexual immorality, impurity and debauchery; idolatry and witchcraft; hatred, discord, jealousy, fits of rage, selfish ambition, dissensions, factions and envy; drunkenness, orgies, and the like"* (Gal. 5:19-21). Look carefully at that list. There is not a single thing there that glorifies God. There is not one item that shows the power of God to a lost world around you. Your life will reflect your decisions. When you choose to please the sinful desires of your flesh, God promises you will reap destruction (Gal. 6:8).

However, when you choose to live by the Spirit, yielding control of your life over to Him, it will be just as obvious, because *"The fruit of the Spirit is love, joy, peace, patience, kindness, goodness, faithfulness, gentleness and self-control"* (Gal. 5:22). Now look again at *that* list. Every one of these things brings honor and glory to God! Furthermore, none of these things are of your own doing. They are the fruit *of* (or belonging to) the Spirit. When these are evident in your life, it's not because you have manufactured the right kind of love or have generated the correct amount of patience or kindness. When there is love, joy, peace, patience, kindness, goodness, faithfulness, gentleness, and self-control being manifest in your life, it is solely because you have fully yielded to the Holy Spirit and *His* fruit is being seen through your daily living!

As we have seen, we are not to allow sin to exercise kingly authority over us in our bodies. We are not to obey its evil longings for pleasure. Paul then goes on to admonish, *"Do not offer the parts of your body to sin, as instruments of wickedness, but rather offer yourselves to God, as those who have been brought from death to life; and offer the parts of your body to Him as instruments of righteousness"* (Rom. 6:13). You cannot prevent sin from persisting to try to maintain control over your body. But, through Christ, you are able to keep sin from *ruling* in your body by making a continuous, conscious choice to offer yourself entirely to God, which includes every part of your body.

Praise the Lord, there is a day coming when you will no longer need to concern yourself with this. As a born-again believer, your *"citizenship is in heaven. And we eagerly await a Savior from there, the Lord Jesus Christ, who, by the power that enables Him to bring everything under His control, will transform our lowly bodies so that they will be like His glorious body"* (Phil. 3:20-21).

To be honest, I can't wait till that day! I can't stand my body right now. No, I'm not referring to my looks, or even my physical shape or condition (although the latter could probably use some help). I just can't stand how it's always working against me. Sometimes the temptations I experience, and the deep cravings for sinful pleasures it presents me with, are almost overwhelming. I understand what Paul means when he says, *"We ourselves, who have the firstfruits of the Spirit, groan inwardly as we wait eagerly for our adoption as sons, the redemption of our bodies"* (Rom. 8:23). What is the *inward groaning* Paul is talking about? It is the new nature crying out for the redemption of, or deliverance from, our sinful bodies so that we can live the life we were created for — glorifying Him.

Until that time though, your body is the *"temple of the Holy Spirit, who is in you, whom you have received from God...you are not your own"* (1 Cor. 6:19). Through the power of the Holy Spirit, because of Christ's sacrifice, you are able to say no to the reign of sin in your body. It is by the Spirit that you are to *"put to death the misdeeds of the body"* (Rom. 8:13). Before you were saved, you *"were controlled by the [flesh], the sinful passions aroused by the law were at work in [your] body, so that [you] bore fruit for death"* (Rom. 7:5). Now that you are born again, you are *"controlled not by the [flesh] but by the Spirit"* (Rom. 8:9). As Paul says, your body is meant for the Lord, and the Lord for the body (1 Cor. 6:13). As you can see, your body already belongs to God, so offering it to Him as a living sacrifice is a reasonable and spiritual act of worship.

Learn to Count with a Beat

Sin no longer has power and dominion over you, dear friend. I know at times it feels like it still does, but understand that is the enemy at work, deceiving your mind. You are now dead to sin — its power over you is gone. Paul says,

> *"We know that our old self was crucified with Him so that the body of sin might be done away with, that we should no longer be slaves to sin — because anyone who has died has been freed from sin. In the same way, count yourselves dead to sin but alive to God in Christ Jesus. Therefore do not let sin reign in your mortal body so that you obey its evil desires. Do not offer the parts of your body to sin, as instruments of wickedness, but rather offer yourselves to God, as those who have been brought from death to life, and offer the parts of your body to Him as instruments of righteousness. For sin shall not be your master, because you are not under the law, but under grace"* (Rom. 6:6-7, 11-14).

I want you to notice that in verse 11 Paul uses the transitional phrase "in the same way." He is saying, in essence, "you must know and fully believe what I've just said, or what I'm about to say will make no sense." So what did he just say?

Your old nature is dead and gone; therefore, sin no longer has dominion over you. Because of Christ's work on Calvary you have been freed from sin! And because this is God's absolute truth, you need to *count* yourselves dead to sin. To "count" means you are taking it to the bank as a fact. God said it, and that settles it.

Now think about this: God says sin can reign in your body, NOT in your nature. Why is this so significant? As we have seen, your old nature is dead and gone, never to come back again. Sin does not and cannot reign there because you have within you a new nature that is incapable of sinning. Therefore, sin resides in your body — in your humanness — and God commands you not to let sin reign in your body. Don't give it any kingly authority over you.

We have also learned that because of your new nature, you have the ability to not sin. Don't forget, through the power of the Holy Spirit your body can be controlled (1 Cor. 9:27). This is why I emphasize so strongly that you don't have to sin. You sin because you choose to; and you choose to because it brings temporary pleasure. You do the things you do because in your heart you want what you want.

Titus 2:11-12 tells us that *"the grace of God that brings salvation has appeared to all men. It teaches us to say 'No' to ungodliness and worldly passions, and to live self-controlled, upright and godly lives in this present age."* Saying "no" to ungodliness and worldly passions, and living a self-controlled godly life is a daily decision you have to make. Not just when you get up in the morning, but all the time. Every instance where you are faced with a temptation, you are also faced with a decision. Do I give in this time or do I continue to stand firm and fight it? Do I yield to the Spirit and glorify God, or focus on myself? You are constantly using your mind throughout each day to make decisions. This is why it is vital that you discipline your mind to say "no" to the flesh and "yes" to the Holy Spirit.

Running the Race

Let's take a close look at what Paul says in 1 Corinthians 9:24-27:

> *"Do you not know that in a race all the runners run, but only one gets the prize? Run in such a way as to get the prize. Everyone who competes in the games goes into strict training. They do it to get a crown that will not last; but we do it to get a crown that will last forever. Therefore I do not run like a man running aimlessly; I do not fight like a man beating the air. No, I beat my body and make it my slave so that after I have preached to others, I myself will not be disqualified for the prize."*

Paul uses a reference here to the Greek games from which we get our modern-day Olympics. The first thing I want you to notice is that Paul likens the Christian life to that of a long-distance runner. We are exhorted to run with one goal in mind: run in such a way as to get the prize. Now, I'm not much of a runner (truth be told, I don't run at all), but I do know that in order to run the distance you have to be in shape.

In verse 25, Paul says, *"Everyone who competes in the games goes into strict training."* In other words, that runner has to train himself in such a way that he is able to control the unfruitful longings and desires of the flesh so that he can accomplish his ultimate goal. If he doesn't, he runs the high risk that those desires are going to get in the way and keep him from reaching his goal. That kind of control involves denying fleshly desires, ignoring the cries of his body for rest, relaxation, and the pleasures of certain foods. The one who trains for the run must constantly push and exert his body, taking it to the limit and beyond — all for the purpose of winning the prize at the end of the race. He knows that if he gives in and yields to the desires of his body, he would not be able to finish the course and win the race.

As a Christian, you should also deny your fleshly desires. You should ignore the cries of your body for sinful pleasures.

Giving in may be enjoyable for the moment, but the long-term ramifications aren't worth it. You should live each day with the understanding that if you choose to yield to the sinful desires of your body, you will compromise your ability to run the race.

Paul goes on to say, *"They do it to get a crown that will not last; but we do it to get a crown that will last forever"* (v.25). The athlete running in a race knows there is the risk that he or she will not win. So they push themselves beyond their limits so that they might win the prize at the end of the race. During Paul's day, the prize was a laurel wreath. Of course, they also received the fame and recognition that came with it, however fleeting it may be.

The exciting thing about the race that Christians are running is that every Christian who applies themselves to careful training, submitting to God's Spirit in our inner man, will win! This is why Paul counsels us to run in such a way as to get the prize. We aren't running for a laurel wreath that will die, or for fame that will fade with time. We are running to receive a *"crown that will last forever."* Paul calls it a *"crown of righteousness, which the Lord, the righteous Judge, will award to me on that day — and not only to me, but also to all who have longed for His appearing"* (2 Tim. 4:8). This is a prize *"that can never perish, spoil or fade — kept in heaven for you"* (1 Pet. 1:4).

"Therefore, since we are surrounded by such a great cloud of witnesses, let us throw off everything that hinders and the sin that so easily entangles, and let us run with perseverance the race marked out for us" (Heb. 12:1). Running this race isn't easy. It requires perseverance through the rough times, seeking the joy of the Lord as our strength. It means that you endure the pain of trials and testing, pushing through it by the power of the Spirit. The only way we can run like this is to go into strict training, just like the athletes. The athlete trains to receive a reward that won't last. But God says that our reward will last forever.

When athletes are preparing for the main event, they place specific restrictions upon themselves. They are careful about their diet, sleep, exercise, and other aspects of their lives. They set up daily routines and do not deviate from them. This isn't something that comes naturally for them. It is a requirement they submit themselves to. It is no different for you and me, dear friend. If you expect to grow and excel in your Spiritual life, you must place specific restrictions upon yourself. You need to be careful about your spiritual diet. What are you allowing to enter your mind through the things you see and hear? Train yourself to be godly (1 Tim. 4:7).

Paul also says we should not live our Christian life without a purpose or goal in mind. *"I do not run like a man running aimlessly; I do not fight like a man beating the air"* (v.26). The person who runs with a purpose is looking straight-ahead to his goal. All of his attention is focused on the finish line. We read in the book of Hebrews that we are to *"run with perseverance the race marked out for us… [fixing] our eyes on Jesus, the author and perfecter of our faith…"* (Heb. 12:1, 2).

The person who runs with a purpose doesn't give up. The person who runs with intent pushes on no matter what. Paul expressed it this way: *"I press on toward the goal to win the prize for which God has called me heavenward in Christ Jesus"* (Phil. 3:14). To "press on" means to run swiftly in order to catch the thing you are pursuing. In other words, don't quit. Don't give up.

Step Into the Ring
Paul then moves his illustration to that of a boxer who is shadow boxing (1 Cor. 9:26). A shadow boxer is "beating the air" instead of hitting an opponent. Although shadow boxing can help a boxer warm up his muscles and get into a rhythm, it does not constitute real boxing. He is hitting the air, not fighting his adversary. Shadow boxing is simply a means of getting ready for the main event. In real boxing, there is a purpose to each blow. Paul's point is this: if all you ever do is spiritually shadow box, if all you do is put on a show for others, you will not know genuine spiritual victory. You need to actually get into the ring

and strike precise blows against your enemy — which, in this case, is your sinful nature.

This leads us to verse 27, where Paul says, *"No, I beat my body and make it my slave."* Why? Because *"in me, that is, in my flesh dwells no good thing"* (Rom. 7:18). If you do not submit control of your body to the Holy Spirit, it will lead you down the path of sin every time (just like the car with its wheels out of alignment). You cannot let your body's sinful tendencies dictate to you what you will and will not do. It must not exercise kingly authority over you.

God's will is that you be sanctified (living a life that is set apart for Him), and He instructs you to learn how to control your body in a way that is holy and honorable (1 Thess. 4:3-4). When you give in to the desires of your flesh, you won't be yielding to the desires of the Holy Spirit and Christ won't be exalted in your body through those actions.

"Do you not know that your body is a temple of the Holy Spirit, who is in you, whom you have received from God? You are not your own; you were bought at a price. Therefore honor God with your body" (1 Cor. 6:19-20). Every Christian is to live a life worthy of the calling we have received (Eph. 4:1). We are commanded to *"purify ourselves from everything that contaminates body and spirit, perfecting holiness out of reverence for God"* (2 Cor. 7:1). This means we *must* take control of our bodies.

Paul uses a very strong term here. He says he "beats" his body. It literally means "to turn black and blue." Now wait a minute, does this mean we should take a whip or bat and literally beat ourselves? Is Paul advocating self-flagellation? Most emphatically not! This concept literally means you are to treat your body with severity, subjecting it to stern and rigid discipline, leaving no room for error. To better understand this, let's make note that we must — as Paul says in Romans 6:19-20 — offer our bodies as a slave to righteousness. When we submit our bodies to the control of righteousness we will reap benefits that lead to holiness.

In other words, you are to deny your body the sinful pleasure it craves. You are to be stern and rigid in the discipline of your body. No matter how much your flesh cries out for satisfaction and fulfillment, if what it craves does not glorify God, you must deny what it wants — submitting the control of your body to righteousness through God's Spirit. That will often involve great difficulty and even, sometimes, pain. This is why Paul uses the term, "beat my body."

Furthermore, Paul writes this in the present tense, active voice, and indicative mood. In other words, every single day (present tense) you need to beat your body and make it a slave to the right desires of the new nature — placing it under the control of the Spirit. You can never let up. And if you don't do it, it's not going to get done (active voice) because no one else is going to do it for you. There is no room for deliberation on this. It's a simple statement of fact (indicative mood).

Can You Do It? Yes You Can!

Here's the exciting thing. As a Christian you have the Holy Spirit dwelling within you, guiding and empowering you. You can indeed do all things through Christ because He gives you the strength and ability to accomplish it (Phil. 4:13).

Paul put it this way: *"If the Spirit of Him who raised Jesus from the dead is living in you, He who raised Christ from the dead will also give life to your mortal bodies through His Spirit who lives in you"* (Rom. 8:11). It is possible to just say "no" to the desires of the flesh. You have the power of the One who raised Christ from the dead living within you! Think about that. The very same power that raised the dead is enabling you to deny the sinful desires of the flesh and make it do that which will glorify God.

God instructed the children of Israel, *"If you do not drive out the inhabitants of the land, those you allow to remain will become barbs in your eyes and thorns in your sides. They will give you trouble in the land where you live"* (Num. 33:55). Compare that with Romans 13:14 where Paul instructs, *"Clothe yourselves with the Lord Jesus Christ, and do not think about how to gratify the desires of the sinful nature (flesh)."* When you allow your mind to think about how to fulfill the desires of your flesh, your body will act accordingly.

Again, it's important to understand that you do not have to sin. You have a choice. When you sin, you are willingly choosing the short-term pleasures of sin (along with the consequences) over the eternal joys of living for God. And when you make that choice — when you choose to sin — you are offering, willingly handing over, your body to sin instead of choosing to be a "living sacrifice" (Rom.12:1).

It's hard to be the master of your body isn't it! In Galatians 2:20, we read the familiar words, *"I have been crucified with Christ and I no longer live, but Christ lives in me. The life I live in the body, I live by faith in the Son of God, who loved me and gave Himself for me."* I want you to notice that Paul refers to the "life I live in the body." This is huge. That life you live in the body you are to live by faith! Why is that so important?

You are not in this fight alone! You don't have to fight against your body without God's help. The question you need to ask yourself is this: Do I believe that God can and will help me have victory over the flesh? Furthermore, do I really want Him to? Too often we yearn for God to just wave His magic wand and make our struggles with the flesh go away, making everything suddenly and miraculously better. Although God could do that, it's not usually how He accomplishes His purpose. God gives us His commands, precepts, and principles within His Word; He expects us to yield to His Spirit as we read, study, meditate upon, memorize, and apply it to our lives.

You must never forget that your mind plays a crucial role in living a life that glorifies God. To glorify God in your everyday

79

living, you must first glorify Him in your every-moment thinking. This is why you are not to even think about how to gratify the desires of the flesh. If you do, you're like that fish playing with the lure (Jas. 1:14-15). When you choose to *"live by the Spirit...you will not gratify the desires of the flesh"* (Gal.5:16). If you want to gain spiritual victory over your sinful flesh, you need to daily make the decision to say "no" to the flesh and "yes" to the Holy Spirit. Live by the Spirit. That is when you will experience victory in glorifying God in your every-moment thinking!

"Do not conform any longer to the pattern of this world,
but be transformed by the renewing of your mind"
Romans 12:2

~ Eight ~
Transformers: Christians Undisguised

As Christians we are to live by the Spirit, surrendering our lives every moment of every day according to the leading of the Holy Spirit. We do that by, first, saying "no" to the constant cravings of our sinful flesh, and saying "yes" to the Spirit's rule in our hearts and minds. And second, by making a drastic change in our thinking process.

God commands us to *"not conform any longer to the pattern of this world, but be transformed by the renewing of your mind"* (Rom. 12:2). To "conform" conveys the idea of putting on a mask so as to appear to those around you as something you're not. When a Christian conforms to the pattern of this world, they adjust their behavior to imitate the traits or features that are characteristic of the unsaved around them.

Now why would any Christian ever want to do that? Let's face it; it's hard at times to be a Christian. Whether in the workplace, at school, in the neighborhood, or even around family, the unsaved can be harsh and cruel. Satan wants you to believe that you need to act like the world to be able to fit into the world. It's a whole lot easier to put on a mask when you're around the unsaved, acting like they do, talking like they do, laughing at the things they laugh at, all so that you don't come under attack for your beliefs.

God strictly commands us not to conform to the pattern of this world. Not to do the things the world does. When you choose to do the things the unsaved do — to act the way they act, to talk the way they talk — you are doing so for the self-centered purpose of gaining man's approval. Paul asks the question, *"Am I now trying to win the approval of men, or of God? Or am I trying to please men?"* He then goes on to declare, *"If I were still trying to please men, I would not be a servant of Christ"* (Gal. 1:10). Our aim, as we live as followers of Christ in this world, must be to please God, not man (2 Cor. 5:9-11; cp. Acts 5:29). God knows what your real motivations are anyway; He *"tests our hearts"* (1 Thess. 2:4). Remember, *"The LORD does not look at the things man looks at. Man looks at the outward appearance, but the Lord looks at the heart"* (1 Sam. 16:7). As God looks at your heart, what does He see?

Because He *can* see the heart, and His purpose in our lives is to refine us to be more and more like Christ, He convicts us and prompts us to choose those things that bring Him glory. As we've already established, those things that bring Him glory, also bring Him — and us — delight, as well as a sense of peace, joy, hope, and confidence in Him. All in all, it is for our good that He sees our heart, that He tests it, because His desire for us is always and only for our good. Why would we want to conform to something that isn't pursuing our good?

Dear Christian friend, don't conform to the pattern of this world. Don't put on a mask and pretend to be what you're not just so that you can "enjoy" life — which is really not enjoyable at all, especially if you've tasted the goodness of God. We are to *"be imitators of God, as dearly loved children"* (Eph. 5:1). To imitate God is to allow the Holy Spirit to live through you.

As a child of God who is loved dearly, you should desire to also be obedient and to *"not conform to the evil desires you had when you lived in ignorance. But just as He who called you is holy, so be holy in all you do; for it is written: 'Be holy, because I am holy'"* (1 Pet. 1:14-16).

The bottom line is that you are a child of God and you belong to Him. When you allow yourself to conform to the world's way of thinking and doing things, you are committing spiritual adultery. James asks the question, *"Don't you know that friendship with the world is hatred toward God? Anyone who chooses to be a friend of the world becomes an enemy of God"* (Jas. 4:4). What choices are you making every day?

Mental Metamorphosis

Paul tells us not to be conformed to the pattern of this world, but instead, to be transformed. The Greek word Paul uses for "transformed" is very interesting, it is *metamorpho-o* from which we get our English word "metamorphosis." A metamorphosis, according to the Merriam-Webster Dictionary, is the supernatural process whereby something changes from one thing into something totally different. It is a marked, complete change not only of appearance but of behavior and character as well.

What makes a metamorphosis so fascinating is that the change takes place *from the inside out!* The most well-known example of a metamorphosis is that of a caterpillar to a butterfly. The caterpillar changes into a butterfly because the nature of a butterfly is already within it. Imagine that you went into your back yard and dug up a large earthworm. Bringing it inside, you set it on the dining room table and proceed to cut out small wings from colorful construction paper. You then lay the wings on top of the earthworm and, using a straight pin, pin the wings to the worm. What would you have? A squirming worm! The reason you do not have a butterfly is because it is not within the nature of the worm to be a butterfly.

The metamorphosis, or transformation, that Paul is talking about is a change in your life that takes place from the inside out. Think about this: What is on the inside of the Christian? Remember our diagram of Chris? As a Christian — a follower of Christ — you have a brand new, holy nature created by God Himself *inside* you. This new nature is who you are at the core of your being. Paul says you are to be "transformed." That which is on the inside — your new nature — is to be lived on the outside. In other words, your everyday lifestyle should be characteristic of your new, holy nature. The things you say, the things you do, the choices you make are all to be in perfect step with the new nature inside of you. If you recall, Galatians 5:16 commands us to *"live by the Spirit."* When you live by the Spirit, your new nature does not stay on the inside.

Look again at Romans 12:2. *"Do not conform any longer to the pattern of this world, but be transformed by the renewing of your mind."* Do not put a mask on when you are around the unsaved and pretend to be like them, rather let the new nature, under the control of the Holy Spirit inside of you, come out and be on display in your daily living — no matter where you are or who you're with. Live transformed!

Paul says we are transformed by the renewing of our mind. How does renewing your mind bring about a transformation that changes you from the inside out? Consider carefully what it means to renew. To "renew" refers to a total and complete renovation — an extreme makeover, if you will. In other words, your mind needs to be thoroughly overhauled. Think about it this way: when you renovate a home you are gutting out the old and replacing it with that which is brand new. God's command is to renovate your mind, to totally remove and completely take out the old thought-process, and replace it with a brand new way of thinking.

Before salvation, your old nature got you into the habit of thinking, "How can I please *myself?*" Every thought was geared toward one thing: Self. That kind of thinking led to a self-centered, self-worshiping kind of behavior. God says that kind of thinking needs to be totally gutted out and replaced with a new way of thinking.

The new nature God placed within you wants you to learn to think, "How can I please *God?*" When your mind is totally focused on how to glorify God in everything you say and do, your heart will desire to please Him, and your behavior will be godly.

Is this new way of thinking automatic for the Christian? Obviously not, which is why we need the Holy Spirit to discipline our minds and renovate our way of thinking. The fact is, *"you were taught, with regard to your former way of life, to put off your old self, which is being corrupted by its deceitful desires; to be **made new in the attitude of your minds**; and to put on the new self, created to be like God in true righteousness and holiness"* (Eph. 4:22-24, emphasis mine). God instructs us to "put off your old self." But what is the "old self" that we are supposed to put off? First, we know what it's not. It is not the old nature. We know that, because the old nature was crucified at the moment of your salvation. And Paul says the old self *is being* corrupted. Since the old nature is dead, it is impossible for it to be presently corrupted. Therefore, the old self is the tendency your flesh has toward sin. It is the sinful desires and fleshly pursuit to please self that your new nature continuously struggles with.

Notice also that Paul says those desires are "deceitful." They are deceitful because they lead you to believe that fulfilling them will be satisfying. They try to convince you that keeping them happy is what life is all about. They are deceiving you, lying to you, and telling your mind untruths. If you are going to renovate your mind, and if you are going to live a life set apart from sin, you must fill your mind with absolute truth. Jesus said that we are sanctified (set apart) by the truth — that which is an absolute, certain, and genuine reality. He then goes on to explain that only God's Word is absolute truth (John 17:17).

Under Construction

Think about it this way: when you renovate a home, you use tools to accomplish the task. When your mind is renovated, what tool is used? Look again at Jesus' prayer in John 17:17 for the answer. He says we are sanctified (set apart from sin) by "the Truth." Jesus is praying, "Father, make your children holy, set them apart from sin by using your absolute truth which is found only in Your Word." The Word of God is the tool the Holy Spirit uses to renovate your mind. Through His counsel, it will change your thinking, thus transforming your life. The Word of God is the primary key to living by the Spirit (Gal. 5:16). Remember, if you are going to glorify God in your daily life, He must first be glorified in your thought life. What you think becomes what you do.

If you were to permit yourself, for even a moment, to *think* about how you can fulfill the desires of your sinful flesh, your life would begin to focus completely upon that as the goal, and the things you say and do would end up striving to achieve that goal. This is why God says clearly that you are not to even *think* about how to gratify the desires of the flesh (Rom. 13:14). Don't forget that Galatians 5:16 says, *"Live by the Spirit; and you will not gratify the desires of the flesh."* It is your responsibility to say "yes" to the Holy Spirit and not let sin reign in your body (Rom. 6:12), and to offer your body to God as a living, continuous sacrifice (Rom. 12:1).

Reflect for a moment on what we've been learning. According to Romans 12:2 you are to undergo a transformation, a spiritual metamorphosis. That which resides on the inside (your new, holy nature) is to be lived out daily. This transformation takes place as God renews (renovates) your mind with His Word through His Spirit. Think about this: If you are going to live by the Spirit, and if you are going to renew your mind and thus renew your life, what is it that you need to do every day? You must be in the Word of God!

The Psalmist, David, considers this same precept when he asks, *"How can a young man keep his way pure?"* He then answers, *"By living according to your word"* (Ps. 119:9). Let's think about that question, and then the answer, so that we can understand what David is saying. First, note that David speaks of a man's *way*. The word "way" refers to the path of life; that which you do each day based upon the decisions you make. So he's asking how we can keep our way of living, the things we do every day, and the decisions we make, pure — free from sin.

The answer is by "living" according to God's Word. The word "living" refers to observing, retaining, treasuring up, and keeping watch as a guard over something extremely valuable. In other words, to keep your decision-making process, and thus your daily lifestyle, free from sin, you need to get into the Word of God (read it), observe what it says (study it), retain that in your memory (memorize it), let it build up inside of you (meditate on it), and then be on the watch as a guard protecting your heart, which is priceless. In short, the Psalmist is telling us that the way to keep your life pure is by daily adjusting your life to the Word of God, not just knowing what it says, but actually doing it. Or as James said, *"Do not merely listen to the word, and so deceive yourselves. Do what it says"* (Jas. 1:22).

David goes on to say in verse 11, *"I have hidden your word in my heart that I might not sin against you."* To "hide" God's Word means to retain it, to store it up as a treasure. If you see God's Word as highly valued treasure, it will be worth digging for and holding on to, and you will actively hide God's Truth in your heart. Consider this question: How does hiding God's Word in your heart keep you from sinning? David answers later in verse 104: *"I gain understanding from your precepts; therefore I hate every wrong path."*

When you are in God's Word, you gain understanding. You become intimately familiar with who God is and what His will is for your life. As a result you will see sin the way God sees it, hating it as He does, for what it is and what it does. This, in turn, brings about change in your life. Your attitude and behavior is transformed because you now hate sin as God hates it. You will make the necessary adjustments in your life that keep you from sinning. My friend, if you are going to live by the Spirit and glorify God in your life, you must know the Scripture.

Praise God we have His Holy Spirit dwelling within us! Jesus told His disciples that it was for their good that He would send His Spirit to them. He said, *"When He, the Spirit of truth, comes, He will guide you into all truth. He will not speak on His own; He will speak only what He hears, and He will tell you what is yet to come. He will bring glory to me by taking from what is mine and making it known to you"* (John 16:13-14; cp. John 16:5-12).

Just prior to making that statement, He promised, *"The Counselor, the Holy Spirit, whom the Father will send in my name, will teach you all things and will remind you of everything I have said to you"* (John 14:26). In other words, as you study the Word of God, the Holy Spirit will help you understand God's Word. He will guide you in applying God's principles and truth to your life. As you follow His leading, applying the Word of God to your life, you will be living by the Spirit. And according to Galatians 5:16, one of the results of living by the Spirit is that you will not gratify the desires of the flesh!

Do You Remember?

I am going to interject two thoughts here. First, in John 14:26, Jesus said that the Holy Spirit will *"remind you of everything I have said to you."* Let's focus for a moment on the word "remind." Simply put, to remind is to cause to remember. If you are going to remember something, you must first of all know it. You cannot remember something you do not already know.

In order for the Holy Spirit to remind you of what God says about how you should live, you must first read, study, and memorize what God says, storing it up as priceless treasure in your heart. The Holy Spirit then takes what you have studied and hidden in your heart, and uses *that* to teach you and guide you.

When tempted with sin, it is often the Word of God that you have treasured in your heart that the Spirit will bring to your mind to confront you with His truth. If you are not in the Word of God daily, you're not equipping your heart and mind with the tools God has offered you in His Word that could be readily available to the Spirit for renovation and transformation. Renewing your mind and changing your living.

The Spirit's counsel is founded on the all-encompassing Truth found in the Word of God. This means that no one should ever say, "The Holy Spirit told me…," or, "The Spirit impressed upon my heart…," if they cannot, or will not, back it up with specific Scripture. Remember, Jesus said that the Holy Spirit *"will not speak on His own"* (John 16:13). In other words, the Holy Spirit will never tell you something that does not find its foundation in the Word of God. The Holy Spirit will always and only speak God's truth, which we can find in God's Word. God will *never, ever* tell you something that is contrary to His Word.

Will the Real Christian Please Stand Up!

We need to take off the disguise and live transformed lives. How exciting to know that change is not only possible but promised to those who yield to the leading of the Holy Spirit as He impresses God's Truth upon you. It is important to understand that you cannot change yourself. *"Can the Ethiopian change his skin or the leopard its spots? Neither can you do good who are accustomed to doing evil"* (Jer. 13:23). True change can only happen as you renovate your thinking, allowing the Holy Spirit to guide you in the understanding, and application, of God's powerful Truth.

The prophet Samuel told Saul that *"the Spirit of the LORD will come upon you in power…and you will be changed into a different person"* (1 Sam. 10:6). It is the same for us today. As you yield to the Holy Spirit, saturating your mind with and choosing to walk in obedience to God's Word, you will be changed into a different person. But you must choose, as Jacob did, to *"get rid of the foreign gods you have with you, and purify yourselves and change your clothes"* (Gen. 35:2).

As you do, the fruit of the Spirit begins to be seen in your life (Gal. 5:22-25). When you *"trust in the Lord and do good"* and you *"delight yourself in the Lord,"* as well as *"commit your way to the Lord,"* God will *"make your righteousness shine like the dawn"* (Ps. 37:3-6). As Christians we are to let that light *"shine before men, that they may see your good deeds and praise your Father in heaven"* (Matt. 5:16).

Lights On!

Jesus declared:

> *"You are the light of the world. A city on a hill cannot be hidden. Neither do people light a lamp and put it under a bowl. Instead they put it on its stand, and it gives light to everyone in the house. In the same way, let your light shine before men, that they may see your good deeds and praise your Father in Heaven" (Matt. 5:14-16).*

You are to let your light shine, but what is this "light" that Jesus is referring to? In the Gospel of John, we read that John the Baptist *"came as a witness to testify concerning that light, so that through him all men might believe. He himself was not the light; he came only as a witness to the light. The true light that gives light to every man was coming into the world"* (John 1:7-9). Just as with John the Baptist, in and of ourselves, you and I are not light. On our own we have no light to shine. In John 8:12 we read, *"When Jesus spoke again to the people, He said, 'I am the light of the world. Whoever follows me will never walk in darkness, but will have the light of life"* (cp. John 9:5). Jesus says, *"I have come into the world as a light, so that no one who believes in me should stay in darkness"* (John 12:46). And in John 12:36 Jesus said to His disciples, *"Put your trust in the light while you have it, so that you may become sons of light."*

When you accepted Christ as your Savior, you instantly became a "son of light." Paul wrote, *"You are all sons of the light and sons of the day. We do not belong to the night or to the darkness"* (1 Thess. 5:5). When you accepted Christ, the truth of Galatians 2:20 took place in your life. You were crucified with Christ and you became a new creation (2 Cor. 5:17). Christ, the

Light of the world, came to dwell within you through His Holy Spirit (1 Cor. 6:19-20). When you live a godly life, when you live by the Spirit, when you put on the new self, you are letting the light of Christ that is within you, shine for others to see.

Paul exhorts:

> *"Therefore, my dear friends, as you have always obeyed — not only in my presence, but now much more in my absence — continue to work out your salvation with fear and trembling, for it is God who works in you to will and to act according to His good purpose. Do everything without complaining or arguing, so that you may become blameless and pure, children of God without fault in a crooked and depraved generation, in which you shine like stars in the universe as you hold out the word of life — in order that I may boast on the day of Christ that I did not run or labor for nothing" (Phil. 2:12-16).*

Working out your salvation does not mean you are living a life dependent upon works to maintain your relationship with God. The question is asked of the saints in Galatia, *"Are you so foolish? After beginning with the Spirit, are you now trying to attain your goal by human effort?"* (Gal. 3:3). You and I were saved by faith, and we continue to live our Christian life by faith (Gal. 2:20). Working out your salvation means that you are being transformed in such a way that you daily live out what's inside of you. You are learning to say "no" to the flesh and "yes" to the Holy Spirit.

Ephesians 5:8 says, *"You were once darkness, but now you are light in the Lord. Live as children of light."* Jesus said that we are the light of the world. We are to *"let [our] light shine before men, that they may see [our] good deeds and praise [our] Father in heaven"* (Matt. 5:16).

We let our light shine when we focus all of our thoughts on how to please God and give our body daily to God as a living sacrifice. You should live out your faith, by the things you say and do, so that others will see who God is and understand His wondrous love for them.

The Holy Spirit lives within you to help you understand God's Word and to guide you in how to apply the truth to your everyday life (John 14:26; 16:13). When you actually apply God's Word to your life, you are no longer just a listener of the Word but a doer. You are a wise man or woman who is building your godly life upon the rock! That, my friend, is living by the Spirit! And when you live by the Spirit you will not gratify the desires of the flesh, because you will no longer be thinking about how to indulge those sinful desires. Instead you will be thinking about how to glorify God.

"Do not merely listen to the word, and so deceive
yourselves. Do what it says"
James 1:22

~ Nine ~
Do Diligence

I must give you a serious word of warning. As you read God's Word, you are going to learn God's truth. But the truths you will discover from the Bible will do you no good. The truths that God will reveal to you within His Word through His Spirit will be totally worthless *if* they are not put into practice.

Remember that we are to build upon a solid foundation. Jesus said the wise man is the one who not only listens to God's Word, but also does what it says. Living a godly life that truly glorifies Him is realized only when you *do* the truth. Reading or listening to it is not enough, God requires more. Paul instructed Timothy to *"correctly handle the word of truth"* (2 Tim. 2:15). Correct handling of God's Word isn't just reading it or listening to it; it's applying it to your daily life. When you read the Scriptures, when you listen to what God is saying *and* you choose to live by what God says because you know Him, then the knowledge of the truth will lead you to godliness. Only then will you be a wise builder. The key will be diligence in doing what the Scriptures teach.

In the book of James we read:

> *Do not merely listen to the word, and so deceive yourselves.*
> *Do what it says. Anyone who listens to the word but does not*
> *do what it says is like a man who looks at his face in a mirror*
> *and, after looking at himself, goes away and immediately*
> *forgets what he looks like. But the man who looks intently into*

*the perfect law that gives freedom, and continues to do this,
not forgetting what he has heard, but doing it — he will be
blessed in what he does. (James 1:22-25).*

It is important to break this text down into bite-sized pieces
so that we may comprehend what James is saying and better
understand how it applies to our own lives.

Deceived by God's Word?

Look again at James' warning in verse 22: *"Do not merely
listen to the word, and so deceive yourselves."* James is referring to
letting God's Word go in one ear and out the other; to not allow
the truths of the Word to sink in to the point where you will be
moved to do something about what you have heard. Merely
listening means you are hearing the words, considering them for
a moment, and then promptly dismissing them as unimportant
or not pertaining to you. In Matthew 7, Jesus called that kind of
person a "foolish man" (Matt. 7:26).

James is telling us that if you merely listen to God's Word
you *will* be deceived. Let me be quick to point out here that
James is not saying that God's Word itself will deceive you. To
deceive means to lie to; to cause to believe something that is
untrue. God's Word is absolute truth, and no lie ever comes
from God's truth (1 John 2:21). Rather, *hearing* the Word of God,
considering what God is saying, and then dismissing it as
unimportant or not pertinent, causes deception. "Oh, I would
never do that!" exclaims the Christian. "I love going to church
and hearing the pastor preach from the Word. I truly enjoy
opening my devotional book every morning at breakfast and
having a little quiet time with the Lord."

I hear you. But let me ask you this: When you hear the
passages of Scripture being read in the sermon or you open your
Bible to the verses associated with the devotional, are God's
words going in one ear and out the other? Sometimes, as the
Scripture is read, your heart may ache with conviction. Other
times it may pound with desire. Or you may find that you are

indifferent. You need to realize that God is speaking directly to you about *your* life and how *you* should be living for Him, and then take those words and apply them to everyday living. If you do not, you are merely listening to God's Word and you are being deceived.

Every time you sit in a Sunday service and listen to the sermon..., every time you attend your adult Bible fellowship or Sunday School class and hear a lesson taught..., every time you go to Wednesday night Bible study or attend a small group Bible study..., every time you have your devotions or turn on the radio to hear your favorite preacher speak..., and every time you open your Bible to read it... you are listening to the Word of God. What you do with what the Holy Spirit reveals to you is critical at this point. If you are not applying to your life what God is showing about your life, you are like a foolish builder who reads the instructions but doesn't bother to follow them. You are *merely listening* and God says you are being deceived.

To be deceived is to be misled, to believe something to be true that isn't. The verb "deceive," as James uses it here, literally means to reckon wrong — to take time to contemplate something, yet draw a false conclusion about it. When we merely listen to the Word of God, we are taking note of what God is saying and yet we are coming to the wrong conclusions about it because we believe something to be true that is not.

The deception comes in when you hear what God is saying and yet determine it doesn't apply to you, or that you don't need to do anything about it right now. When you hear God's Word and conclude it does not apply to you — at least not at this time — or that it is not relevant to your life, you believe something to be true that is not. Again, it's like a builder who looks at the blueprints and then decides he doesn't need them — his house will stand just fine on its own. The fact is, it probably will — for a while — adding to the deception that all is well. Until the storms of life arrive.

To keep from being deceived, you must actively put into action in your life the things you hear from and see in God's Word. You must choose to live it out daily. When you say you believe the Word of God to be true, but your actions — or lack of action — prove otherwise, you are that foolish man building his house on the sand — deceived into believing his home will stand even in the fiercest storm.

We cannot merely listen to God's Word and go merrily on our way. We must do what God says. Note that James uses the words "do" and "doer" in verses 22 and 23. They carry the idea that you are putting in the required effort. You are actually making something happen. In other words, you are not merely listening to God's Word — you are taking what it says, applying it to your life, and making it happen. You are like the wise builder of Matthew 7.

Mirror, Mirror

James goes on to tell us that if we do not do what the Bible says, we are like a man who looks at his face in a mirror and sees something wrong (Jas. 1:23-25). Have you ever looked in the mirror and noticed your hair all messed up or an unwanted spot on your face? What do you do about it? In James' example, that person has seen in the mirror that a problem exists. He acknowledges it's there and he understands that there is a problem needing to be dealt with, but for some unknown reason, he chooses not to take care of it right then and there. He goes on his way, fully intending to deal with it later. Yet other things, such as the everyday activities, pressures, and demands of life, enter in and vie for his attention.

The result is that he forgets the problem is there and thus doesn't deal with it. James says he is deceived. Even though he fully plans on taking care of it, he walks away and promptly forgets what the mirror has revealed to him. He takes the time to consider it, concludes that it needs to be dealt with and that he will indeed take care of it, but does not. He comes to a wrong conclusion — which is proven by his lack of action.

By just listening to the Word of God and not acting on what the Holy Spirit has shown you and convicted you of right then and there, you are drawing a false conclusion. You are building your house on the sand. You understand that what you read is true, "Here is an area of my life that I need to deal with, and I will." But if you don't address it right then and there, you've been duped by the enemy, my friend.

Consider this: When God reveals an area of your life that needs addressing and you choose not to attend to it immediately, that area will get worse. Just like an open sore, left unattended it will fester and grow. It will be harder to deal with later. It is critical to face head-on whatever God reveals to you. Immediately. Don't wait!

James speaks of the one who "*looks* at his face in a mirror and, after *looking* at himself, goes away" (Jas. 1:23-24, emphasis mine). The verb "look" means to perceive, to observe and understand, to consider attentively as you are fixing your gaze upon something. "To look" simply means that you see the problem and are fully aware that it's there. The mirror of God's Word has revealed it to you and you have fixed your gaze intently upon it. Remember, both the wise man and the foolish man had read God's Word — they both looked into the mirror. It's what they did with what they saw that made the difference.

The trouble lies not in the identification of the problem but in the execution of the solution. Instead of immediately dealing with what the mirror revealed, this individual simply identifies that the problem exists and then "goes away." He turns and walks away from it. Now, I think it's fairly safe to say that if you saw a big zit glowing at the end of your nose, you would immediately address the issue. It wouldn't even cross your mind to walk away until it was dealt with. Yet, the person James is talking about sees something much more severe than acne, and yet he still turns and walks away without dealing with it.

In verse 24 we see that the moment he goes away he *"immediately forgets what he looks like."* He has forgotten what the mirror revealed to him. Here, the word "forget" means that you are neglecting something, no longer caring for it. The fact that he *no longer* cares for it suggests he did, at one point, care — at least to a certain extent when it was originally revealed to him. Something else has come in and drawn his attention away. He has turned his focus away from it and on to other things that have suddenly become more important. The result is that he has begun to care more for that other thing instead — forgetting the imperfection that he had seen in the mirror.

By the way, the fact that he no longer cares for it does not mean that it's unimportant to him. He didn't see the problem in the mirror and say, "Nah, no big deal." It's not that he didn't care *about* it, but that he did not take the time right then and there to care *for* it — to attend to it. He simply began to focus his thoughts onto something else and thus put his energy into attending to other things instead.

When you read the Bible and the Holy Spirit does reveal an area of your life that you need to work on, I'm sure you don't respond with "no big deal." You agree that it's something you need to take care of. But if you don't care for it right then and there, you've drawn a wrong conclusion. This is how merely listening to the Word can deceive you.

As you study the Scriptures, the Holy Spirit will reveal something to you — something you need to work on. You see it and respond with, "WOW! I need to do something about that!" And yet you decide to wait and address the problem later. At that moment, you have drawn a false conclusion that you will take care of it at another time. Oh dear friend, when the Holy Spirit speaks to you, don't look into the mirror of God's Word, see an issue in your life that needs to be dealt with, and then turn and walk away. I urge you to deal with it right then and there. Whatever appointment you may have to get to, whatever thing you are planning to do, can wait. In the whole scheme of things, they pale in importance compared to the priority of having your heart right with God. Don't risk walking away from that mirror and forgetting what God showed you in His Word. Later may be too late.

James goes on to say in verse 25, *"But whoever looks intently into the perfect law that gives freedom, and continues in it — not forgetting what they have heard, but doing it — they will be blessed in what they do."* God says you are to "look intently" into His Word. This means to stoop to a thing in order to look at it closely; to look at it with your head bowed forward and chin up, body leaning so as to get as close to the mirror as you possibly can for the purpose of becoming thoroughly acquainted with the details of what the mirror has revealed.

Furthermore, you do not stand in a darkened room to look in the mirror, you turn a light on. Without the light you cannot see the blemish so as to properly take care of it. Not only is God's Word a mirror, it is also a *lamp* to our feet and a *light* to our path (Ps. 119:105). God's commands are radiant, giving light to the eyes (Ps. 19:8). When you open the Bible and open your heart to the Holy Spirit, your secret sins will be exposed in the light of His presence (Ps. 90:8).

You see, the unfolding of God's Word gives light, revealing to us those things that are hindering a deeper relationship with Him (Ps. 119:113). The bottom line is this: God's commands are a lamp, His teaching *is* light (Prov. 6:23). Every time you open the Bible, every time you read the Scriptures, every time you are exposed to God's truth, you are coming into the light (John 3:21). And that light will expose, as if in a mirror, the issues you need to deal with (Eph. 5:13-14).

Let's say you're standing in front of your bathroom mirror when you notice what appears to be a dark smudge on your chin. You immediately stop what you were doing and lean forward, as close to that mirror as you can, so that you are able to get a much better look at that spot and determine what to do next. The picture James is painting is that of a person looking into the mirror of God's Word and seeing a spiritual blemish. God has revealed an area or aspect of his life that needs to be changed. As a result he stops everything he's doing and leans closer to the mirror to get a better look at it. In other words, he searches the Scriptures and studies God's Word to learn more about that issue in his life and how he should address it. As the Holy Spirit guides him into the truth, he discovers that there really is a matter of concern that needs dealing with. He immediately addresses the blemish right then and there. God says that man is a blessed man.

By the way, to immediately address the blemish is more than just confessing that sin before God. It begins there, but also involves eradicating it from your life completely and applying the Word of God in such a way that you are altering your lifestyle so as to never accommodate that sin again. For the sake of illustration, let's say that you look in the mirror and see a blemish on your cheek. You clean it up, apply some ointment on it, and then go on your way. Over the next few days you periodically look in the mirror to see how it's doing. You may have to clean it up again and put more ointment on it. As you continue to tend to it, it eventually heals and goes away. To address your spiritual blemish requires more than just confession. It involves going to the Word of God, finding God's truths that apply to that issue in your life, studying the Word, memorizing it, meditating upon the truth, and living by it every day.

You are to look intently into the Word of God. You are not just to give it a passing glance but get close to it, so close that you can examine the details of what it is showing you. God has much to reveal to us in His Word. Within the pages of Scripture we find God's truth about who we are, who He is, and how we are to live that godly life we are seeking after. At times that means His Word is going to show you things that need to be dealt with: maybe a nagging sin that needs to be removed once and for all; or an attitude that needs to be changed; or a thought-process that needs adjusting. A cursory glance at the Bible will not usually reveal those things to us. It is when you look intently into His Word that you will see your true reflection.

It is the Word of God we are instructed to look intently into. I know there are a lot of great books by great authors on how to live for God, how to have a closer relationship with God, and how to have victory over sin. But without the Word of God filling your mind, you will not know true victory. Satan doesn't care if you quote Spurgeon, or MacArthur, or Stanley, or any other of a long list of great Christian authors, as long as you're not using the Word of God. God's Word is the "perfect" law of liberty. It is complete. It is all we need, nothing else. And you are to look intently into it. We are to *invest* time in studying, not just spend a few minutes glancing at the Word of God. When we do, and when we apply what the Holy Spirit has revealed to us, that is when we are "blessed." That is when we know true happiness.

Notice James' use of the word "and" in verse 25. Specifically he writes *"whoever looks intently into the perfect law that gives freedom, and continues in it."* This word "and" is called "a conjunction of annexation." A conjunction of annexation takes two separate things and unites them, making them totally dependent upon each other. In other words, you cannot have one without the other. For example, you've probably heard of peaches and cream or peanut butter and jelly. Here's what James' use of that word "and" is telling us: not only must you "look intently" into the Word of God (search the Scriptures), you must also "continue" in it (live it out in your daily life). These two events are totally dependent upon each other. You must not merely listen to the Word; you must also apply it to your life and do what it says. When you live your life this way, you will be like that wise man or woman who builds their house on the rock.

Every day you are to be in the Word of God. Every day you are to look intently into the Scriptures. Every day you are to contemplate God's truth and do what it says. You are to walk in obedience consistently and constantly. As you look intently into God's Word, the Holy Spirit will reveal to you the blemishes of your life that need to be dealt with so that every word and every deed glorifies your Heavenly Father (Col. 3:17).

"Seek first His kingdom and His righteousness, and all these things will be given to you as well"
Matthew 6:33

~ Ten ~
Prosperity and Success:
Kingdom and Righteousness

It is probably safe to say that most of us want to be prosperous and successful, whether it is at work, in our financial endeavors, as well as marriages and friendships, and on the list can go. Is there anything wrong with that? Of course not. However, we must keep in mind that prosperity and success, as the world defines it, is not to be our primary goal.

The most important aim of every Christian is to know God and to honor and glorify Him with every aspect of their life. Scriptures make it clear that whatever we do, we are to do it all to the glory of God (1 Cor. 10:31; Col. 3:17). To do this, you must begin by carefully examining your priorities. Ask yourself these questions:

- What is most important to me?
- What drives me throughout the day?
- What excites me?

The bottom-line is that your answer reveals where your priorities lie and where you will put the majority of your attention and energy. If you are putting your life's emphasis on anything other than glorifying God and knowing Him, you will fail to achieve your ultimate goal.

The Dethroning of King Me

In Matthew 6:33, Jesus says you are to *"Seek first His kingdom and His righteousness, and all these things will be given to you as well."* Consider carefully what Jesus is saying. First and foremost, the things you are to seek after are God's kingdom and God's righteousness. The problem is that in our self-centeredness you and I are trying to build our own little kingdoms, seeking a different "king" to reign in our lives is low on our priority list.

We tend to put self on the throne daily. We try to manufacture events and control circumstances in such a way that we are able to experience constant happiness and satisfaction. As a result, we become a slave to self — all of our thoughts and energies are directed toward fulfilling the will of "King Me." Occasionally, we may even try to fit a thing or two of God's into our already-packed agenda, thinking that we are doing well. Yet God says the way to true contentment, peace, and godliness is by dethroning "King Me" and seeking *His* kingdom and *His* righteousness for our lives — His rule, His authority — as our highest priority.

Think about the verb "seek." In Matthew 6:33, it is a word that carries the idea of craving something so much that you focus all of your thought and attention on finding it, so as to acquire it. It's like a heat-seeking missile that, when fired, has a singular target or goal and won't stop until it reaches it. Nothing can deter it from its purpose. Just like that missile, you are to seek after God's kingdom and righteousness to reign in your life. In other words, you seek after it at any cost — bending your entire will toward getting it, submitting yourself to the pursuit of it.

There are a lot of things out there that you can seek after — money, prestige, fame, happiness, pleasure, etc. — yet, out of all the things you could seek for and occupy yourself with, God says you are to seek *first* His kingdom and His righteousness. That is your primary target.

It is important to emphasize that Jesus uses this verb "to seek" in the present tense, active voice, and imperative mood. If you recall, when something is written in the present tense, it represents a simple statement of fact that is occurring in actual (or real) time. In other words, it is happening right now; it is happening right now; it is happening right now — constantly, never ending, always in real-time. When God uses the present tense to command us to seek His kingdom and righteousness first, He is telling us that this is something we are to never stop doing. We are to moment-by-moment and day-by-day focus all of our thought and attention on submitting to God's kingdom and righteousness in our daily lives.

Second, when something is written in the active voice, it means that *you* are doing the action. You have to do it; no other human being can do it for you. God's command to seek His kingdom and righteousness is given to you specifically. It is something that you alone must be constantly doing every day of your life. I cannot do this for you, nor can you accomplish this task for me.

Now, the exciting thing is that we do not do this in our own power. If we did, it would end up being all about us instead of God. Don't forget that our ultimate goal is to do everything for God's glory. As Paul declares in Philippians 4:13, we can do all things through Christ who gives us the strength. As you submit to Him, the indwelling Holy Spirit gives you the power, ability, know-how, and desire to seek His kingdom and righteousness in your life.

Finally, the imperative mood simply means that it is a command. When God gives a command, our response and responsibility is simple: obey. If you choose to not obey, or to delay obedience, you are sinning (1 John 3:4). Do you grasp the impact of this? If you are not daily, actively focusing your will, thoughts, and actions toward submitting to God's kingdom and righteousness ruling your life, you are sinning! You are defiantly disobeying God. You are like that foolish person trying to build a godly life on shifting sand (Matt. 7:24-27).

Look at Matthew 6:33 again, and let's piece this back together. Jesus says you are to *"Seek first His kingdom and His righteousness, and all these things will be given to you as well."* This is a command that only you can do; and you must be doing it in real-time — every moment of every day. The Holy Spirit will guide and empower you, as you choose to constantly pursue, first and foremost, God's kingdom and God's righteousness as the authority for your life. It is not impossible. We can declare right along with the apostle Paul that *"I can do everything through [Christ] who gives me strength"* (Phil. 4:13).

Finally, we must note that to seek first God's kingdom and righteousness means this: you are denying your selfish desires while craving after and pursuing His rule, His will, and His authority in every aspect of your life — in your public life, and in your private life. Whether it is at work, at home, at the mall, out on the golf course, at the beach, or on vacation — wherever you may be and whatever you may be doing — you are to seek first God's kingdom and righteousness in that event or place.

Seeking God's kingdom and righteousness involves completely immersing yourself in the understanding of His will and walking in total obedience — in the strength of the Holy Spirit — to your Lord at all times, as you desire to know Him more and more. Before being prosperous or successful in any other endeavor, you should desire, more than anything, to be prosperous and successful as a Christian — by striving, in every aspect of your life, to seek first God's kingdom and righteousness. Only then will you experience true prosperity and success. And then you will be able to say with the Apostle Paul, *"I consider my life worth nothing to me; my only aim is to finish the race and complete the task the Lord Jesus has given me..."* (Acts 20:24).

Have You Made It?

What is true prosperity and success? The world would say it's achieved when you have a happy marriage, your kids all honor and respect you, you have a solid position at work along with a six-figure income, you're a pillar in the community, your bank account is growing, and you're enjoying great health. While all those things define the American dream, they are not necessarily God's definition of prosperity and success. We tend to make everything about us. But it's not. It's all about God.

Look at how the King James Version renders Joshua 1:8. *"This book of the law shall not depart out of thy mouth; but thou shalt meditate therein day and night, that thou mayest observe to do according to all that is written therein: for then thou shalt make thy way prosperous, and then thou shalt have good success."* Notice that God tells Joshua that when he meditates daily on the Scriptures, *then* Joshua would make his way prosperous and enjoy good success. It is only when you meditate on God's Word, applying its truth to your daily life, that your choices to glorify God will affect a lifestyle change. You are making your "way," — your course of life — prosperous. It is then that the contentment, peace, and godliness God has promised to you will be experienced in your life.

The word "prosperous" refers to achieving your goal. Remember, the goal of the Christian is to know and glorify God in everything we say and do. When you meditate daily on God's Word, applying its truth to your everyday living, and seeking to know Him more, you are changing the course of your life. You are achieving your ultimate goal. You are being truly prosperous. Prosperity isn't about achieving the great American dream and having it all. It's about living a life that glorifies God, day in and day out. When you are living that kind of life, you are experiencing all that God has planned for you.

Another by-product of meditation on God's Word is that you will "have good success." The word "success" literally means that you have been given insight and comprehension into *who*

God is and what His will is for your life. The direct result of this insight is that you are able to act wisely in your every-moment choices. Success isn't found in gaining that promotion at work. Success is experienced only when you know God more and choose those things that will bring honor and glory to your Heavenly Father — succeeding at that which He created you to do.

Prosperity and success, as God defines it, can only be achieved as we meditate on His Word. We are to *"read it all the days of [our] life so that [we] may learn to revere the LORD [our] God and follow carefully all the words of this law and these decrees"* (Deut. 17:19). We are to *"delight...in the law of the LORD, and on His law...mediate day and night. [Then we will be]...like a tree planted by streams of water, which yields its fruit in season and whose leaf does not wither. Whatever [we do] prospers"* (Ps. 1:2-3).

Eat Your Vegetables and Say Moo

God instructs Joshua to *"not let this Book of the Law depart from your mouth; meditate on it day and night, so that you may be careful to do everything written in it. Then you will be prosperous and successful"* (Josh. 1:8). God reveals three things we must do in order to experience true prosperity and success.

First, eat your vegetables. No, I'm not referring to carrots, corn, and green beans. But there is an analogy I would like to draw from that. Do you eat? Of course you do. We all eat. But why do you eat? I know that we can come up with many different reasons, but the bottom line is that as we eat, the nutrients from the food we consume help us grow and gain weight.

Bend your left arm up at the elbow and feel your bicep. Now feel the bones in your wrists. The nutrients that come from food help our bones and muscles grow and stay strong. Stand up and do a couple of jumping jacks (you probably need the break by now anyway). Those same nutrients give us the energy we need (carbohydrates) to go throughout the day. They also help us stay well and get well quickly when we get sick. The fiber in our food helps us digest food and helps keep our teeth and gums healthy. It is also equally true that if we eat "junk food" all the time, our bodies will suffer.

Ok, why the health-break? Paul told Timothy that *"physical training is of some value, but godliness has value for all things"* (1 Tim. 4:8). It is important for our physical well-being, health, growth, and development to not only eat food but eat the right kinds of food. It is even more important for your spiritual well being, growth, and development that you not only "eat," but eat properly. God instructs Joshua (and us) to keep His Word on our lips. In other words, you need to daily feed on God's Word. You need a daily diet of Scripture. You need to open your Bible every day and devour the words of your Heavenly Father. Jeremiah said, *"When your words came, I ate them; they were my joy and my heart's delight"* (Jer. 15:16). You need to be in the Word of God every day. There is no way around it.

Second, you must be meditating on God's Word day and night. It is not enough to simply have a quick devotional at the breakfast table or just before going to bed. It definitely is not enough to just listen to the pastor preach the Word on Sunday. You need to be daily reading and studying God's Word, and then throughout the day, continuously focusing your thoughts on what you have read. Did you read your Bible today? Do you remember what you read? Have you been thinking about how it applies to you throughout the day? Have you been asking God to show you how to live it out in whatever you may be doing? This is what it means to meditate.

The meditation God says we are to do is not some mystical, Eastern religion-based event involving sitting cross-legged on the floor with eyes closed, tips of your fingers touching, and chanting to yourself. The verb "to meditate" in Joshua 1:8 refers to breaking something down into small chewable pieces. This, in turn, makes it easier to digest and get it into your system so that you can draw strength and nourishment from it — similar to a cow chewing her cud. But consider this: that cow can't chew her cud until she has first eaten some grass. Make sense? If there is no grass in her stomach, there will be no cud to chew. In the same way, it is impossible for you to meditate on God's Word if you are not first studying it. You must *feed* upon the Word before you can meditate upon it.

After sufficiently chewing the grass, the cow swallows it, sending it into the first of four chambers in her stomach. Similarly, when you have your devotional time, or sit in church and follow in your Bible as it is being taught, or whenever you are reading the Scriptures, you are feeding upon the Word of God. You are chewing on it and then swallowing it, taking it in storage for later use.

I've been told that up to 70% of cows chew their cud when they are *resting*. In other words, they are bringing up that grass they ate earlier in the day and chewing on it again at a later time. As the cow chews, she is breaking the grass down even further, swallowing it into the second chamber of her stomach. A little while later she will bring it up again and chew on it some more. Each time she is breaking it down further to enable proper digestion.

How does this apply to you and me? Let's say you've read some Scripture during breakfast — you have fed upon God's Word. As you progress through the morning you begin to think about what you read. You think about what it means, about how it applies to your life, about how you should adjust your actions. The Holy Spirit begins to show you how to understand some basic concepts and principles from God's truth. During your lunch break, you sit there eating your leftover ham between two slices of dry bread while thinking more about that text from the Bible and what the Holy Spirit has revealed to you. You are definitely seeing that God is showing you an area of your life that needs some attention. You utter a prayer asking your Father to reveal to you what He wants for you and to give you the strength to apply it to your life. That evening someone makes a comment that upsets you and immediately that verse of Scripture you've been meditating on through the day pops into your mind. Smiling, you reply with a Biblical, loving response instead of the retort you would have given yesterday.

Do you understand the process of meditation? That was a much-simplified example, but the bottom line is that you start by reading the Word — feeding upon it. Then periodically throughout the day, you bring it back to mind and think about it, evaluating, scrutinizing, seeking to know and understand how it applies to you. You keep your heart open to the leading of the Holy Spirit, asking Him to guide you into God's truth. As you chew on (meditate upon) the Scripture you begin to understand the principle God is teaching you and you see how you can, and should, apply it to your life. Then God gives you practical opportunities to apply what you have learned. This is the process of meditation.

Let's go back to the illustration of a cow chewing her cud. I've been told that dairy cows spend almost 8 hours a day chewing their cud for a total of almost 30,000 chews daily. That is a lot of chewing! How much do you meditate on God's Word? How many "chews" a day do you have? It's been said that a contented cow is one who is seen chewing her cud. I believe it would be safe to say that contented Christians are those who are meditating faithfully upon God's Word. *"Do not let this Book of the Law depart from your mouth; meditate on it day and night, so that you may be careful to do everything written in it. Then you will be prosperous and successful"* (Josh. 1:8). I'd say Joshua is describing a contented Christian, wouldn't you?

Allow me to remind you that *what* you meditate upon is crucial. You are to meditate upon the Word of God which is flawless (Prov. 30:5), living and enduring (1 Pet. 1:23), as well as active and powerful (Heb. 4:12), and, as a result, it is at work in believer's lives (1 Thess. 2:13). It continues to spread and flourish even today (Acts 6:7; 12:24). It helps us stay pure (Ps. 119:9) and keeps us from sin (Ps. 119:11). It provides us with a spiritual compass (Ps. 119:105) and is useful for teaching, rebuking, correcting, and training in how to live a righteous life, as well as equipping us for every good work (2 Tim. 3:16-17).

God's Word is what you are to meditate upon, hiding it in your heart and thinking deeply about it during the day. You must allow the Holy Spirit to guide you into all truth (John 16:13), and give you wisdom and strength as you purpose to live it out each day. As you do, you are seeking first His kingdom and His righteousness.

What do I DO?

The third requirement that must be met for true prosperity and success in the Christian life, according to Joshua 1:8, is walking in obedience to what God's Word says. Notice that God instructs Joshua to *"be careful to do everything written"* in His Word. Think about that little word "do." What does it mean to *do* something? It seems like a silly question, yet we know that every word of God is inspired and thus important (2 Tim. 3:16). The verb "do" in this verse is written in the imperfect tense. In other words, this is an action that is incomplete. It is not finished. It must, therefore, continue on into the future. Obedience to God's Word is an ongoing action. You are never done with doing what God says you should do.

You see, as you read Scripture and meditate on God's truth, the Holy Spirit will reveal to you how you are to live in pursuit of God's kingdom and righteousness. He will show you how to build your godly life upon a solid foundation. It is not enough to just read the Bible, you must then do what God says (Jas. 1:22). If you just read the Word but do nothing about it, you're like that foolish man who tried to build his house on beachfront property without building it upon a solid foundation (Matt. 7:26-27).

What I am sharing with you throughout this book is not some magic pill which promises that you will no longer have problems or trials or painful times in your life if you swallow it.

This isn't a special formula that offers you a happy marriage, wonderful children, a six-figure income, great health, and never having to experience serious temptation if you follow it. Remember, that kind of result is how the world defines prosperity and success.

What we are exploring and pursuing is how to live a life that reflects glory to God. We are discovering from God's own words how to please and honor Him. He promises that as you learn to focus on His Word and obey Him — relying on the strength and counsel of His Spirit — you will know true prosperity and success the way He defines it. God says, *"Obey me, and I will be your God and you will be my people. Walk in obedience to all I command you, that it may go well with you"* (Jer. 7:23).

*"Blessed is the man who fears the LORD, who finds
great delight in His commands"*
Psalm 112:1

~ Eleven ~
Delighting in God's Word

I am going to ask you a question. Ultimately the answer requires you to be brutally honest with God. Are you ready? Here it is: How do you *feel* about God's Word? "What?" you may ask. "You're kidding me, right?" Nope. I'm quite serious. How do you feel about God's Word? Assuming that your answer is something like, "I love God's Word!" let me ask you this: Do your actions support that answer?

The psalmist writes that the one who experiences true happiness is the one *"whose delight is in the law of the LORD, and who meditates on His law day and night"* (Ps. 1:2 NIV). To experience true happiness — to be blessed of God — we need to "delight" in the law of the Lord. God does not say here that you will be blessed if you appreciate His Word, nor if you merely respect it. We are to delight in it.

"To delight" means to find great pleasure in something to the point where you are longing for it constantly. I can remember back in college when my wife and I were dating. As I got to know her, I found myself constantly thinking about her. Every moment we were apart was sheer agony. I couldn't wait until class was over and I could be with her again. The long walks just talking were pure heaven. I hung on to her every word. The more I learned about her, the more I wanted to know and the more I wanted to be with her. I truly delighted in her.

Today, nearly 30 years later, every moment we're apart my heart aches. It's true! Every time my Instant Messenger dings with an IM from her my pulse increases. I can't wait for the workday to be over so that we can be together again. I look forward to sitting at the dinner table and listening to her as she tells me about her day. Even today I'm still learning things about her I never knew. The more I learn about her, the more I want to know and the more I want to be with her. I am so privileged, honored, and humbled to be able to say I still delight in my wonderful wife!

God says you are blessed when you delight in His Word. You should long for the time each day when you can sit down with your Bible and listen to your Father speak to you. You should go throughout each day anxiously looking forward to the moments when you can sit down with your Bible and cling to His every word. The psalmist writes, *"Blessed is the man who fears the LORD, who finds great delight in His commands"* (Ps.112:1). If you really want to know God's blessing on your life, find great delight in His Word! Again the psalmist says, *"Direct me in the path of your commands, for there I find delight...I delight in your commands because I love them...if your law had not been my delight, I would have perished in my affliction"* (Ps.119:35, 47, 92).

This truth became very real to me a few years ago. There was a time in my life when I turned my back on God. I chose to pursue the pleasures of sin for a season, not wanting anything to do with God. Because of that choice, I nearly lost my family and my life. During those dark days, my wife and I went to numerous "Christian" counselors, but nothing seemed to help. That is, until we began meeting with a couple from our church.

This couple, who have now become dear friends, began taking us deep into the Word of God. Each time we met, we invested our time in seeing what God had to say about our situation and how He had the answers we were searching for. Each time we met, we were challenged to read the Scriptures during the week, and we were given verses to memorize.

During those weekly sessions, the Holy Spirit awoke within me a deep desire to study my Bible every day. I began hungering and craving for more. I relished every moment I could invest in reading God's Word. I discovered verse after verse that spoke to my heart's issues and I committed them to memory. I also found myself looking forward to the times each day when I could focus my thoughts in prayer and talk with God about the things He had revealed to me.

Today I am still excited about the Word of God. I am passionate about reading God's truth and hiding His principles in my heart. I get excited every time the Holy Spirit shows me another precept, and I am able to dig into my Bible to compare Scripture with Scripture. This is what it means to delight in God's Word.

You see, it wasn't until I began digging into the Word of God, studying the Scriptures, meditating on them, and memorizing them, that true change started happening in my life. Digging into God's Word and getting to know God more required action, no one else could do it for me — it was personal. It is personal. This book is a direct result of the journey God has taken me on. This isn't just a series of lessons for me to teach, I believe in this with all my heart. This is what the psalmist is talking about when he says, *"If your law had not been my delight, I would have perished in my affliction"* (Ps.119:92).

Had I not begun to study, memorize, meditate on, and seek to obey God's Word — and if I don't continue to do it even now — I would still be gripped by my sin. I would be perishing in my affliction. Truly delighting in God's Word means you are going to invest your time in it, you are going to study and memorize and meditate upon it, as well as walk in obedience to it. As a result you will find great peace and direction in the midst of your greatest conflicts. That is God's promise!

We need to say as Job did, *"I have not departed from the commands of [God's] lips; I have treasured the words of His mouth more than my daily bread"* (Job 23:12). And we should echo the words of Jeremiah when he said, *"When your words came, I ate them; they were my joy and my heart's delight"* (Jer. 15:16). Is your testimony that of the apostle Paul who said, *"In my inner being I delight in God's law"* (Rom. 7:22)?

Delighting 101

The pressing question we have to face here is this: How do we get to that point? What must I do in order to experience true delight in God's Word? It begins with a personal relationship with Jesus Christ. The unsaved don't care for the God of the Word, so they won't care for the Word of God. They don't see the need for it. They don't understand it. And until they have a personal relationship with Christ, they aren't going to. Do you know for certain where you will spend eternity? Do you know Jesus Christ as your personal Lord and Savior? This is the first step toward delighting in God's Word. This is the first step to true happiness, prosperity, and success.

Second, before we can truly delight in God's Word we must understand that the Bible is not just another book. It is not some novel you pull off the shelf and read all the way through in a weekend. It's not a storybook, although it tells the story of God's redemptive love for mankind. It is not a romance novel, although it shares the account of how God demonstrated His love for man by sacrificing Himself on our behalf. It is not a history textbook, although it does tell the history of mankind from creation to His eternal destination. Neither is it a how-to book for do-it-yourselfers, although it shows us how to live a life that brings glory to God.

The Bible is God's Word written to you and me to show us who God is and who we are before Him. It also shows our need for a Savior, and God's provision through the person of Jesus Christ. In the Bible we see God's desire to have a personal relationship with us — and within its pages He shows us how we can know Him, not just as Creator and Judge, but as Savior and Father and friend. The Bible teaches us how to live lives that are holy and pure. It shows us how to say no to sin and yield our lives to full and complete surrender to God — living a life that truly glorifies Him. Oh, my friend, it is vital that we invest our time in the Word of God daily.

I challenge you right now: take a close look at your life — its ups and downs, blessings and trials. Life is hard. The Bible is God's Word given to help you cope with every issue of life you will ever face. As you yield to the direction of the Holy Spirit, it helps you deal with temptations, handle life's trials and testing, and teaches you how to find peace and contentment through an intimate relationship with your Father. The Bible is the instrument God uses, as His Spirit works in you, to provide you with power and strength, understanding, wisdom and knowledge, hope and peace. Within the pages of Scripture is life and food for your soul. Can you begin to understand why you need to delight in God's Word?

I want to make it clear that Bible study, in and of itself, does not automatically cause us to glorify God in our lives. You won't glorify the Lord simply because you know more and study more from the Scriptures. You must open your heart and surrender to the message of God's Word and the One who wrote it. You must not be merely listeners, but doers of the Word as well. We must address the issues of sin that God reveals to us. We must choose daily to open God's Word, submit to God's leading through His Spirit, seek His will, and walk in obedience to Him. This is what is life-changing.

Do you want to live a life that glorifies God? Live according to the Word of God (Ps. 119:9). Do you want to live a sin-free life? Hide God's Word in your heart (Ps. 119:11). Do you need to find strength and encouragement during times of stress, suffering, and sorrow? Read God's Word and let it uplift you (Ps. 119:28, 50). Do you feel lost and need a sense of direction? Open your Bible and let God guide you (Ps. 119:105). Are you looking for hope and protection? You'll find it in the Scriptures (Ps. 119:114, 147). When you see God's Word in this light, you can say with the psalmist, *"I delight in your decrees; I will not neglect your word"* (Ps. 119:16).

Looking again at Psalm 1:2, we note that the blessed man delights so much in God's Word that he *meditates* on it day and night. Not only does he long to open God's Word to read it, he thinks about what he read all day long. Remember, the one who is meditating on God's Word is feeding upon it and then bringing it back up again later to chew on it some more. The one who is meditating on Scripture is thinking deeply about what God has said and how it applies to his or her life. When you are truly delighting in God's Word, you are going to do more than just read it — you're going to meditate upon it and you are going to apply its truths and principles to your daily living.

By the way, "meditate" in Psalm 1:2, is written in the imperfect tense, meaning that it is an action that is not yet completed. It is something that must be repeated again and again and again. When you delight in the Word of God you just can't ever get enough of it. Listening to it just isn't adequate. Reading it doesn't suffice. You find yourself meditating on it throughout the day. You think about it again and again, praying about it, speaking it, longing to understand its depths.

To be prosperous and successful in your Christian life you need to delight in and meditate upon the Word of God. Do I sound like a broken record yet? I make no apologies. We need to read God's Word daily, as well as break it down and chew on it throughout the day. We are to think about it all day long and then act upon what it says.

For Your Consideration

David wrote Psalm 119 as he was considering the benefits of God's truth to his life. In verse 15 he writes, *"I meditate on your precepts and consider your ways."* In this verse, the word "consider" refers to having your thoughts focused; much like a laser beam is focused light. A laser beam is far more powerful than regular light. So it is when we *consider* God's Word. When you focus your thoughts upon Scripture you can accomplish much. Your mind may begin to wander — which can get you into trouble. Yet, as you submit those potentially distracting thoughts to God — seeking to focus on the Word He has directed you toward, you will find that He will give you strength to continue considering Scripture and focusing your mind on knowing God's Word and doing God's will (Col. 3:2). Delighting in the benefits of God's truth is accomplished when you are meditating on what He has revealed to you.

Now look at verse 97 where the psalmist declares: *"Oh, how I love your law! I meditate on it all day long."* A moment ago I asked if you delight in God's Word like Paul did. Now I ask, do you *love* God's Word? The word "love" in this verse refers not to simply enjoying or liking something a lot, but rather having a large appetite for it. It is craving something so much that all you can think about is getting hold of it so you can have it. David cries, *"I love your commands more than gold, more than pure gold"* (Ps. 119:127). What earthly treasure do you value more than anything?

> Seriously reflect on these questions:
> How much do you love God's Word?
> Are you "considering" it during the day?
> Are your thoughts focused upon it?
> Does the Word of God permeate your thinking like a laser beam all day long and into the night?
> When you encounter an unplanned-for situation, what are your first thoughts?
> When a boss is demanding or a client is frustrating you, when the children aren't obeying or the car breaks down in the middle of rush hour, what goes racing through your mind?
> When you're home all alone, what do you allow yourself to think about?

When you delight in God's Word, the truths of Scripture fill your mind and direct your thoughts. When you delight in God's

Word, you are always seeking first His kingdom and His righteousness.

Again in Psalm 119, notice in verse 148 that the psalmist says, *"My eyes stay open through the watches of the night, that I may meditate on your promises."* When you can't sleep at night, what do you think about? The psalmist encourages you to truly meditate on God's Word. He reminds us to let the promises of God occupy our thoughts. You see, my friend, the Holy Spirit uses the Word of God to direct your thoughts, and that is going to make a difference in your life. But let me remind you of this crucial point: you cannot meditate on God's Word if you are not studying it and memorizing it (Ps. 119:11).

In this study we are discovering the power of the Scriptures in affecting lasting change in our lives — change that will enable us to bring glory to God in all we say and do. God says His Word is to be fixed in our hearts and in our minds (Deut.11:18). We know God takes His Word very seriously. We should take His Word seriously also.

Do you want to be prosperous and successful? Do you want to build a godly life upon a solid foundation? Understand that when the law of God is in your heart, your feet will not slip (Ps. 37:31). When you hide God's Word in your heart, you won't sin against Him (Ps. 119:11). The fact is, the Word of God is to be in you "richly" (Col. 3:16). And as you meditate on His Word day and night, you will be prosperous and successful (Josh. 1:8); you will be wise men and women building your homes upon a rock (Matt. 7:24-25).

When you are *"careful to do what the LORD your God has commanded you;"* when you *"do not turn aside to the right or to the left;"* when you *"walk in obedience to all that the LORD your God has commanded you,"* then you will *"live and prosper and prolong your days"* (Deut. 5:32-33).

*"Above all else, guard your heart, for it is
the wellspring of life"*
Proverbs 4:23

~ Twelve ~
Understanding the Mind

In Bible times, the fountains and wells were watched over with extra special care. That water source was their lifeline. If something got into the well to taint the water, it could have significant impact on their lives. They cooked with it, they drank it, and even their flocks drank from it. Nothing was allowed to enter that well if it had the potential to be harmful. As long as the water in the well was clean and pure, life was good.

Your mind plays a very important role in being godly. To allow sinful thinking is to pollute your entire life. Have you ever stopped to consider what things around you, in your daily environment, have impact upon what and how you think? The things you see and the things you hear have a direct influence on the things you think. The things you think determine the things you do. Therefore, what you see and what you hear have a strong influence on your daily activity.

Remember what we learned from Colossians 3:17. Whatever you say and do is to glorify God. Of necessity then, whatever you allow yourself to see and hear must also glorify God. If it does not, you must refuse to see it or listen to it because it can have a powerful impact on your mind — thereby impacting your actions — leading you to make self-centered decisions and self-focused actions. My friend, this isn't something to be considered lightly.

Proverbs 4:23 says, *"Above all else, guard your heart, for it is the wellspring of life."* The words "above all else" refer to having a faithful, unwavering, and focused commitment to something — far more than you do to anything else. It means that this thing takes highest priority. Nothing should be more important to you than to have a faithful, unwavering, focused commitment to guarding your heart.

What is the purpose of a guard? Simply put, a guard keeps watch for the enemy. He understands that the enemy is nearby, he wants to destroy you, and can attack at any moment. The guard is posted to protect the camp; sounding the alarm and giving the call to arms should the enemy approach. An effective guard is always on high alert.

In Proverbs 4:23 we are commanded to guard our hearts above all else. The heart is so much more than where your emotions occur. The word "heart" here is the Hebrew word *leb* (pronounced Leh-bay) and refers to your understanding or seat of knowledge. In other words, it is your mind. It is the place of your intellect. It is the place where all of your thinking and decision-making happens. It is the starting point of everything that you say and do, and you are to place a constant guard over it. Why is it so crucial that our highest priority is to guard our minds? The answer is found in our verse, *"Above all else, guard your heart [mind], for it is the wellspring of life."* *Everything* you do flows from everything you think!

Your thoughts determine the kind of life you will live. Just like the fountains and wells in ancient times could be tainted, affecting the community water source, so also allowing sinful thoughts can pollute your entire life. This is why it is of highest importance that you set a constant guard over your mind. If your thoughts are pure and holy, the things that you do will be just and good. If you allow sin to taint your thinking, your actions will not glorify God. From your mind springs the decisions of life.

Equipped with that understanding, let's look at Proverbs 4:23 again. "Above all else (with an unwavering and focused commitment), guard your heart (protect the place where reasoning, thinking, and decision-making occurs), for it is the wellspring of life (how you live flows from what you think)" (addition mine).

If you are going to glorify God in your daily life, He must first be glorified in your thought life. This isn't just a quaint or cute little saying that I keep repeating over and over again. This comes from the very mouth of God as a mandate for every Christian — *above all else*! You are to faithfully, unwaveringly have a focused commitment on setting a guard of protection over your mind because from your thoughts come your actions. Do you get the idea that God wants you to be serious about what you think? This is a clear-cut warning to be constantly and consistently on our guard regarding what we allow to enter our mind.

Are you going to be a listener or a doer (James 1:22)? If guarding your mind is not your highest priority, it needs to be — now. As you have looked at the mirror of Scripture in Proverbs 4:23, has God revealed a blemish in your life? You need to decide what you will do about it. Are you going to sit here and say, "Wow! Good point," and do nothing about it? If so, then God says you're deceiving yourself. Not because you're choosing not to listen to me, but because you've chosen to ignore His Word.

Here's what I encourage you to do right now. Set aside this book, get a pen and paper, and begin writing a course of action using these questions to help you: 1) How are you going to deal with this blemish that God has revealed? 2) What steps are you going to take *right now* to set up that guard of protection over your mind? Don't wait. Don't allow yourself to think, "I need to do this, but I'll do it later" (see James 1:22, review chapter 9). If you do that, you are only deceiving yourself. God says that guarding your mind must be your highest priority. Oh, dear friend, deal with it now.

Once you've taken the first step and have written a plan of action, take the next step and begin to put it into place. One of the purposes of this book is to help you do that. The most effective way I've found to set a guard over my mind is to memorize scripture. Possibly you have already memorized Psalm 119:11. If not, I encourage you to do so. It says, *"I have hidden your word in my heart that I might not sin against you."* Setting a guard over your mind begins with the Word of God! It begins by memorizing Scripture. It begins by hiding verses like Colossians 3:17, 1 Corinthians 10:31, Colossians 3:2, and Proverbs 4:23 in your heart. This is God's own plan for protection!

Monkey See – Monkey Do

It is vital that you be very careful about what you allow your eyes to see. What you see affects what you think, and what you think becomes what you do. Every day you are faced with choices about what you're going to permit yourself to see. Are you going to choose to see only those things that encourage you to live a godly life, or will you allow things that tempt you to indulge in the lusts of the flesh?

If you want your life to glorify God, the Scriptures are clear that what you fill your mind and heart with make the difference. For example, speaking of *"those who follow the corrupt desire of the sinful nature"* (2 Pet. 2:10), Peter says, *"With eyes full of adultery, they never stop sinning"* (v.14). What you see affects what you think, which in turn affects what you do. If your focus is on ungodly, sinful things, you will never stop sinning.

In the Sermon on the Mount, Jesus said, *"The eye is the lamp of the body. If your eyes are good, your whole body will be full of light. But if your eyes are bad, your whole body will be full of darkness"* (Matt. 6:22-23). Jesus used the word "lamp" to refer to something that shows the body which way to move. In other words, what you see has a direct impact on what you do. If your eyes are good, if they are focused on the things that will glorify God, then the deeds you do will also glorify Him. But if you allow yourself to see things that are ungodly, your lifestyle will reflect that choice.

You need to make decisions about what you will read, watch, or even what you will listen to. Are there certain types of media that God has put His stamp of approval on? Are there others that He has definitively said not to watch? The answer is yes, but not in the way you might expect or desire it. Paul challenges us to *"be very careful, then, how you live — not as unwise but as wise, making the most of every opportunity, because the days are evil. Therefore do not be foolish, but understand what the Lord's will is"* (Eph. 5:15-17).

God does have a will for you in what you should see and what you shouldn't, and you are to understand what that will is. But you will not find a listing anywhere that says, "Thou shalt watch these things and thou shalt not watch those." Wouldn't it be so much easier if God published "The Throne's Weekly Theatre Reviews: Heaven's Movie Guide" to show you which movies received His two-thumbs-up? Instead, God expects us to exercise godly wisdom and discernment — which the Holy Spirit gives to us through God's Word. God says that *"a discerning man keeps wisdom in view, but a fool's eyes wander to the ends of the earth"* (Prov. 17:24).

The way you discover God's will for what you should or should not see is to be a student of God's Word. As you become intimately familiar with the Author of Scripture, it will become easier for you to understand the voice of the Holy Spirit as He directs you to discern between things that are going to help you grow spiritually and those that can draw you away from God, thus weakening your faith.

Now consider this: we are instructed in Philippians 4:8 that our minds should be thoroughly occupied with things that are true, noble, right, pure, lovely, and admirable. Since what you see has a direct impact on what you think, then it stands to reason that the things you see should also be true, noble, right, pure, lovely and admirable. (I will expand more on Philippians 4:8 in chapter 14.)

Yes, we are living in the age of Grace, and as Christians we have great freedom, but keep in mind that *"You, my brothers, were called to be free. But do not use your freedom to indulge the sinful nature"* (Gal. 5:13, emphasis mine). You still must always be careful about what you allow your eyes to see. Be very wary about what you allow yourself to watch. King David cried out to God to help him, *"Turn my eyes away from worthless things"* (Ps. 119:37). Things that are worthless are things that hold no eternal value, and they are things we should not focus our attention on.

You need to *"be careful to lead a blameless life...walk in [your] house with a blameless heart...set before [your] eyes no vile thing"* (Ps. 101:2-3). When we place vile things in front of our eyes (that which is good for nothing, unprofitable, and can lead to destruction), we are also exposing our minds to those things. With enough exposure, your mind will become accustomed to what you are seeing, and your thought process will be altered. This, in turn, will modify your behavior. This is why God instructs His children to *"get rid of the vile images you have set your eyes on"* (Ezek. 20:7).

What do you allow to be watched on the television in your home? Think about the movies you permit to be viewed. David said, *"No one who practices deceit will dwell in my house; no one who speaks falsely will stand in my presence"* (Ps. 101:7). Now I know that some of you will argue with me about this, claiming that it's just harmless entertainment, and that you know the difference between what's going on in a sitcom and what's real. But let me challenge you to carefully consider the things you are watching. Are you allowing those who practice deceit and speak falsely to stand in your presence? Are you letting your eyes see things you shouldn't, exposing your mind to things that are harmful to it?

Paul urges you *"to watch out for those who cause divisions and put obstacles in your way that are contrary to the teaching you have learned. Keep away from them"* (Rom. 16:17).

I'm not saying you should never watch television or see a movie. I'm also not saying that you should never play computer games or the like. I am saying, as Paul did, that you should *"test everything. Hold on to the good. Avoid every kind of evil"* (1 Thess. 5:21-22). Look at that word "test." It means literally, to scrutinize intently with the purpose of approving it. That verb is written in the present tense, active voice, and imperative mood. In other words, you are to consider carefully that TV program, movie, website, or computer game and test it (examine, analyze, and dissect it). Determine if its content glorifies God. Not just once, but constantly (present tense). You are not to rely on others to do it for you (active voice), this is your responsibility. This isn't an option for the Christian, it is God's command (imperative mood). If it passes inspection, great. If not...avoid it like the plague!

Dear Christian brother and sister, *"Do not love the world or anything in the world...for everything in the world — the cravings of sinful man, the lust of his eyes and the boasting of what he has and does — comes not from the Father but from the world"* (1 Jn. 2:15-16). Remember, the world desires for its offerings to be viewed as pleasurable. The world's intention is to cause you to like it, enjoy it, and eventually embrace it. But *everything* in the world is *not* from God. If it does not bring honor and glory to God, I should have nothing to do with it.

Your very first test for what you allow your eyes to see should be this: *"Love the Lord your God with all your heart and with all your soul and with all your mind and with all your strength"* (Mark 12:30). In the final analysis, anything you see that takes your love and focus away from God, from His Word, and from doing His will, doesn't belong in your life.

If you do not guard your heart, by being careful of what you allow yourself to see, the deception of Satan will slowly creep in and warp your thinking, pulling you away from God. You need to *"drive out the inhabitants of the land, those you allow to remain will become barbs in your eyes and thorns in your sides. They will give you trouble"* (Num. 33:55).

As Paul declared, *"Bad company corrupts good character"* (1 Cor. 15:33). What kind of company are you allowing into your home and into your mind through the television and movies, or via the computer? If you allow your eyes to see that which does not glorify God, you are allowing your mind to think on things that do not glorify God. And this will result in a life that does not glorify God. "Oh, be careful, little eyes, what you see!"

If you haven't yet made the same commitment as David did, to *"set before my eyes no vile thing"* (Ps. 101:3), then I challenge you to commit right now. Review everything you allow your eyes to see, including TV, movies, the Internet, video games, books, magazines, and the like. If it does not bring glory to God, don't look at it. Period. Make the decision today to say, *"My eyes are ever on the LORD, for only He will release my feet from the snare"* (Ps. 25:15).

Wearing Blinders

Proverbs 4:25 counsels, *"Let your eyes look straight ahead, fix your gaze directly before you."* The verb, "to look," refers to paying close attention to something, considering it very carefully. In other words, you should pay close attention to what you see, considering very carefully the things that your eyes are observing, because what enters through the eye-gate influences what you think. Again I will ask the tough, but important, questions that demand an answer:

> What do you allow your eyes to see?
> What kind of images do you look at?
> Where do your eyes linger?
> What kind of books and magazines do you read?

What types of TV shows and movies do you watch?
What websites are you frequenting?

Every one of those things has a powerful influence upon your mind.

God says to look "straight ahead." This means your focus is to be directly in front of you, not to the left or the right. This is figurative, not literal. In other words, God isn't saying it's wrong for your eyes to literally look left or right. If that were so, I doubt He would have created us with the ability to look around. So what is He saying?

Let's compare Scripture with Scripture by looking at similar statements. In Joshua 1:7, God tells Joshua to *"be strong and very courageous. Be careful to obey all the law my servant Moses gave you; do not turn from it to the right or to the left, that you may be successful wherever you go."* In this verse, God uses the phrase, "do not turn from the right or to the left," to communicate the importance of staying faithful and true to His Word. Don't allow yourself to deviate from it. God says in Deuteronomy 28:14, *"Do not turn aside from any of the commands I give you today, to the right or to the left, following other gods and serving them."* Again, God's instructions are very clear. *"Be very strong; be careful to obey all that is written in the Book of the Law of Moses, without turning aside to the right or to the left"* (Josh. 23:6).

Let's look at Proverbs 4:25 again, in light of these verses and our understanding of the meaning of *"look straight ahead."* The command from God is, *"Let your eyes look straight ahead, fix your gaze directly before you."* Your focus, your attention, all that you think about, is to be centered upon the Word of God and the will of God. When this is the center of your attention, God alone will influence and direct your thinking. The Holy Spirit will guide you in how to affect your behavior to bring glory to God.

When you focus on that which is directly in front of you, like the blinders on a horse, you will not be distracted by other

131

things that have the potential of taking you off the right path. You won't see that lure dangling enticingly off to the side, trying to draw you away from your single-hearted devotion to Christ. Deuteronomy 5:32 says, *"Be careful to do what the LORD your God has commanded you; do not turn aside to the right or to the left."* God is very clear, our eyes are to look straight ahead at all times. In Psalm 141:8 the psalmist declares, *"My eyes are fixed on you, O Sovereign LORD."* The one who should always be directly in front of us is Jesus!

I find great significance in the fact that our eyes are to look "straight" ahead. The psalmist prays, in Psalm 27:11, *"Teach me your way, O Lord; lead me in a **straight** path"* (emphasis mine). His prayer is that God would instruct him on the direction he should be going (teach me your way). That instruction comes as we feed upon the Word of God. Notice also that he asks God to lead him, to guide him, in a straight path. I submit that the only path God will ever lead you down is the straight one. His promise is, *"I guide you in the way of wisdom and lead you along straight paths"* (Prov. 4:11).

The reason Proverbs 4:25 tells us that our eyes should look straight ahead is because that is where God is! And that is the direction where God is leading. When you keep your eyes fixed on God, when your gaze is always looking straight ahead, this is what will happen:

> *"For the LORD gives wisdom, and from His mouth come knowledge and understanding. He holds victory in store for the upright, He is a shield to those whose walk is blameless, for He guards the course of the just and protects the way of His faithful ones. Then you will understand what is right and just and fair — every good path. For wisdom will enter your heart, and knowledge will be pleasant to your soul. Discretion will protect you, and understanding will guard you. Wisdom will save you from the ways of wicked men, from men whose words are perverse, who leave the straight paths to walk in dark ways, who delight in doing wrong and rejoice in the perverseness of*

evil, whose paths are crooked and who are devious in their ways. " (Proverbs 2:6-15)

You may be familiar with what Proverbs 3:5-6 says: *"Trust in the LORD with all your heart and lean not on your own understanding; in all your ways acknowledge Him, and He will make your paths straight."* Compare that with Proverbs 4:25. Keep your focus on God. He will make sure you are walking the straight path, the path that will glorify Him. Investing time in the Word of God every day will provide you with wisdom. It will give you an understanding of what is right, just, and fair. It will show you every good and straight path.

God's Word will give you discretion and understanding. It will keep you from looking to the left or to the right, which would tempt you to leave the straight path. Proverbs 15:21 says that *"a man of understanding keeps a straight course."* Keep in mind, though, that simply reading God's Word is not enough. God will show you in His Word the path you are to take; you must choose moment by moment to actually walk it. Paul says that when we decide to walk the path that the Holy Spirit shows us (from God's Word), that is when we will not gratify the sinful desires of the flesh (Gal. 5:16).

Do You Hear What I Hear?
Not only does what you see have a direct impact on living a life that glorifies God, but so is what you hear. You must have a faithful, unwavering, focused commitment to guarding your mind from being attacked by the things you hear. Proverbs 23:12 tells us to apply our ears to words of knowledge. Proverbs 2:2 says to turn our ears to wisdom. Those verbs, "to apply" and "to turn," indicate a conscious effort on your part to be aware of everything you hear, disciplining yourself to listen to only that which glorifies God.

What you allow yourself to listen to plays an important role in living a God-centered life. Romans 10:17 tells us that *"faith comes from hearing."* If you want your life to reflect your faith in

God, then you should be careful about what you allow yourself to hear. Hear only those things that will help to build your faith rather than tear it down. Proverbs 18:15 says, *"The heart of the discerning acquires knowledge; the ears of the wise seek it out."* Your ears should be tuned only to those things that will glorify God.

You should never allow yourself to hear *"obscenity, foolish talk or coarse joking, which are out of place, but rather thanksgiving"* (Eph. 5:4). Look at what Christ says in Mark 4:24, *"Consider carefully what you hear."* Christ used the word "consider" to say this: turn your thoughts to what you hear, weighing every word carefully. You must be careful about what you allow yourself to listen to, whether it's on the radio, on TV, or in the movies, at school, work, or talking with family and friends. What you hear affects what you think, and what you think becomes what you do.

I should also note that the verb, "to consider," in Mark 4:24, is written in the present tense, active voice, and imperative mood. Sound familiar? Every moment of every day you are personally responsible for what you hear. You are personally accountable to God for what you choose to listen to. Doesn't it stand to reason that every day of your life you should be careful about what you expose your thinking to? As I said earlier, we are instructed in Philippians 4:8 that our minds are to be thoroughly occupied with things that are true, noble, right, pure, lovely, and admirable. Since what you hear has a direct impact on what you think, then it stands to reason that the things you listen to should also be true, noble, right, pure, lovely, and admirable.

If a TV show or movie begins to use foul, vulgar language, turn it off or get up and walk out of the theatre. Not after the fourth time, not after the third time; don't allow it to go on past the first time. If it happened once, it's likely to happen again. Paul exhorts us in Colossians 3:8 to *"rid yourselves of all such things as these: anger, rage, malice, slander, and filthy language from your lips."* Does it not stand to reason that if I am not to be doing these things, then I shouldn't be exposing my mind to them either?

I challenge you to follow a plan that helped me: for the next month keep a journal of everything you watch, read, or listen to. Record what, when, where, how long, and what the content was. Then in one month from now, sit down with a godly Christian brother or sister and ask them to review that list with you. Talk about it. Make adjustments to your viewing and listening habits as God reveals His will.

Guarding the Gates

Your eyes and your ears are gateways into your mind. What you allow to enter through either gate will impact your effectiveness for Christ. Above all else, you must guard your mind. This necessitates guarding your eyes and your ears as well.

Look again at Proverbs 4:25 and take note that God says to "fix" your gaze on that which is directly in front of you. To "fix" your gaze means you are locking something down, setting it — as in cement. In other words, your eyes should not wander at all. You are to look straight ahead — focus on God — and fix (lock) your gaze there. Set your focus on God, my friend, and never wander from Him, no matter what lure may be trying to get your attention. Don't look to the left or to the right. That is not where God is. That is not the place of peace and blessing.

Hebrews 12:2 encourages us to *"fix our eyes on Jesus, the author and perfecter of our faith."* Deuteronomy 11:18 commands us to fix God's words in our minds and in our hearts. 2 Corinthians 4:18 tells us to fix our eyes not on what is seen, but on what is unseen. And Hebrews 3:1 commands us to fix our thoughts on Jesus. Do you get the idea that what you think about — everything that goes on in your mind — matters to God? God's command is clear: fix your eyes and ears on Him. Set a guard around your mind by being very careful about what you see and what you listen to.

King David declared, *"I lift up my eyes to you, to you whose throne is in heaven. As the eyes of slaves look to the hand of their master, as the eyes of a maid look to the hand of her mistress, so our eyes look to the LORD our God ..."* (Ps. 123:1-2). The slave never knew when his master would beckon him, need his service, or require him to do something. So he always kept his eyes focused on the master's hand. The slightest gesture would bring him running. His ears were attentive to the slightest whisper or cough, bringing him instantly to his master's side. If his eyes wandered, or ears focused on other sounds, he would miss the will of his master. In the same way, you and I must be ever diligent to keep our eyes and ears focused on our Savior and Lord.

Proverbs 20:12 says, *"Ears that hear and eyes that see — the LORD has made them both."* Your eyes *and* ears should be always focused on seeing and hearing only that which glorifies God. You cannot have your eyes on both the things of God and ungodly things. They are two separate masters (see Matt. 6:24).

God, in speaking to the prophet Ezekiel, gave him these instructions: *"Son of man, look with your eyes and hear with your ears and pay attention to everything I am going to show you, for that is why you have been brought here"* (Ezek. 40:4). You and I are here to bring honor and glory to God in everything we say and do. In order to do that, we need to pay attention (with both our eyes and ears) to *everything* that God is going to show us. To do that, we cannot — we must not — focus our attention anywhere else.

Are you going to be like those Jesus described in Matthew 13 whose *"heart has become calloused; they hardly hear with their ears, and they have closed their eyes. Otherwise they might see with their eyes, hear with their ears, understand with their hearts and turn ..."* (v.15)? Or will you be like Jesus' disciples of whom He says, *"Blessed are your eyes because they see, and your ears because they hear"* (v.16)? The choice is yours (Josh. 24:15).

~ Thirteen ~
The Master Deceiver

Isaiah says that God *"will keep in perfect peace him whose mind is steadfast, because he trusts in you"* (Isa. 26:3). What a glorious promise! When your mind is completely focused upon God, having total confidence in Him no matter what may be happening around you, God promises to keep you in a place of complete safety. A place where you are able to experience a quiet contentment and soundness of mind. All because you are trusting in Him.

That peace is described in Scripture as *"the peace of God, which transcends all understanding."* A peace that *"will guard your hearts and your minds in Christ Jesus"* (Phil. 4:7). The one *"who trusts in the LORD, whose confidence is in Him …will be like a tree planted by the water that sends out its roots by the stream. It does not fear when heat comes; its leaves are always green. It has no worries in a year of drought and never fails to bear fruit"* (Jer. 17:7-8).

This is why Satan's strategy is to attack your mind. What you think becomes what you do, and Satan knows that if he can successfully get you to listen to and believe his lies, he will be able to lead you away from a *"sincere and pure devotion to Christ"* (2 Cor. 11:3).

Single-hearted devotion, as we explored in Joshua 1:7, indicates that your mind is totally focused on God not self! If you have "single-hearted devotion" to Christ, your life is going to glorify God and point others to Christ. To keep God from being the focus, your enemy is going to wage an all-out attack on your mind.

Paul says, *"We are not unaware of his schemes"* (2 Cor. 2:11). We do not have to go into this battle ignorant of the tactics the enemy is going to bring into play. What strategy is Satan likely to use in his attacks on your mind? James warns us to *"not merely listen to the word, and so deceive yourselves"* (Jas. 1:22). That is exactly what Satan wants to do to us. He wants us to be deceived. In fact, we find in the Bible that Satan is a master at deception. Jesus said that Satan does *"not [hold] to the truth, for there is no truth in him. When he lies, he speaks his native language, for he is a liar and the father of lies"* (John 8:43-44). Revelation 12:9 says that Satan is *"that ancient serpent...who leads the whole world astray."* Satan is a master at deception.

No one knows that better than Adam and Eve. The Scriptures tell us:

> *"Now the serpent was more crafty than any of the wild animals the LORD God had made. He said to the woman, 'Did God really say, 'You must not eat from any tree in the garden'?' The woman said to the serpent, 'We may eat fruit from the trees in the garden, but God did say, 'You must not eat fruit from the tree that is in the middle of the garden, and you must not touch it, or you will die.' ' 'You will not surely die,' the serpent said to the woman. 'For God knows that when you eat of it your eyes will be opened, and you will be like God, knowing good and evil.' When the woman saw that the fruit of the tree was good for food and pleasing to the eye, and also desirable for gaining wisdom, she took some and ate it. She also gave some to her husband, who was with her, and he ate it. Then the eyes of both of them were opened, and they realized they were naked; so they sewed fig leaves together and made coverings for themselves" (Gen. 3:1-7).*

Did you ever stop to consider Satan's strategy in the garden and what we might be able to learn from it? Remember, he is a master at deception. When Satan sought to lead Adam and Eve into sin, he started by attacking Eve's mind. Paul warned, *"I am afraid that just as Eve was **deceived** by the serpent's cunning, your minds may somehow be led astray from your sincere and pure devotion to Christ"* (2 Cor. 11:3, emphasis mine). Note that Eve was deceived by the cunning, subtle craftiness of Satan. And God warns us that even today our minds may be led astray by that same deceit.

Satan used simple steps to deceive Eve and get her to believe his lie. He began with a seemingly innocent question. *"He said to the woman, 'Did God really say, 'You must not eat from any tree in the garden'?"* (Gen. 1:3). I find it very interesting that Satan didn't actually deny that God had spoken. He didn't try to get Eve to believe that God never actually said anything of importance. He simply posed a question — a question that cast doubt: "Did God really say what you think He said? Maybe you were mistaken. Maybe you just misunderstood Him." This attack was subtly geared to merely cast *doubt* upon God's Word.

Look at Eve's response:

> *"The woman said to the serpent, 'We may eat fruit from the trees in the garden..."* (Gen. 3:2).

We can see that the seed of doubt has already begun to sprout in Eve's mind. Look carefully at what she said. Now compare it with what God *actually* said:

> *"And the LORD God commanded the man, 'You are free to eat from any tree in the garden...'"* (Gen. 2:16).

If you look carefully at these two verses, you will notice that as Eve began to doubt God in her mind, her thoughts caused her to actually take away part of God's Word. Can you see which word she omitted? She didn't use the word "free." God had said they were free to eat from any tree in the garden.

Potato, Potatoe

What is so significant about a word as simple as "free"? To answer that question we need to start by taking a look at a statement Jesus made in Matthew 5: *"Do not think that I have come to abolish the Law or the Prophets; I have not come to abolish them but to fulfill them. I tell you the truth, until heaven and earth disappear, not the smallest letter, not the least stroke of a pen, will by any means disappear from the Law until everything is accomplished"* (Matt. 5:17-18; cp. Luke 16:17).

Note that Jesus refers to "the smallest letter" and "the least stroke of a pen." The King James Version uses the words "jot and tittle." The "jot" (smallest letter) refers to the Hebrew letter *"yodh."* It is the smallest of all letters in the Hebrew alphabet, and would occupy proportionately about the same amount of space as that of the English apostrophe. Although the "jot" is the smallest Hebrew letter, it is as important as any other letter.

Think about it this way: Letters spell words; Words compose sentences; Sentences make God's promises. How you spell a word is important. The spelling of a word determines the meaning and purpose of that word.

For example, the word "spring" has a specific meaning. But if we spell that word a different way, even if we change only one letter, we get a totally different word. For example, remove the "g" and replace it with a "t" and you get an entirely different word. "Sprint" has a totally different meaning from the word spring. Single letters change words and their meanings. Jesus' promise in Matthew 5 is that not one jot, not a single letter would fail. Every word is inspired of God, which means that every letter is inspired as well (2 Tim. 3:16). God says what He means and He means what He says — every letter of it.

Jesus also talks about the "least stroke of a pen" (the tittle). A tittle is even smaller than a jot. Whereas the jot is a whole letter, a tittle is only part of a letter. The presence of a tittle forms a specific letter. If the tittle is absent, then it is a totally different letter.

For example, the Hebrew letter *beth* looks like this (figure 5). The Hebrew letter *kaph* looks like this (figure 6). If you look carefully you'll notice one minor difference between these two letters. That little extension on the lower right of the *beth* is called the tittle. If the tittle is present, then it is the letter "*beth.*" If the tittle is not there, then it is the letter *kaph*. And don't forget that every letter is important!

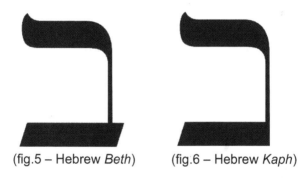

(fig.5 – Hebrew *Beth*)   (fig.6 – Hebrew *Kaph*)

Let me give you another example. The Hebrew letter *daleth* looks like this (figure 7). Whereas the Hebrew letter *resh* looks like this (figure 8). Again notice that the tittle is that little extension on the top right of the *daleth*.

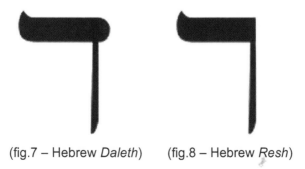

(fig.7 – Hebrew *Daleth*)   (fig.8 – Hebrew *Resh*)

Think about this, we just established how important an individual word is. Each word is made up of specific letters. So a word spelled with the letter *beth* is going to be different than a word spelled with a letter *kaph*. Similarly, a word spelled with the *daleth* is going to have a different meaning than one spelled with a *resh*. The tittle is what determines which letter it is going to be.

Now let me show you an example from our English language (see figure 9). Let's begin with the word FUN. Obviously this word has a specific meaning which most of us can readily identify. When we add a simple "tittle" to the first letter, we have the word PUN which has a totally different meaning. As you can see, that small tittle totally changed the word and its meaning. Now let's add one more tittle to the first letter in this word, and we have the word RUN — a word that has yet another different meaning. Can you begin to see how important a tittle is?

FUN

PUN

RUN

(fig.9)

The point here is this: Jesus declared that all of God's promises would be fulfilled precisely as they were spelled out — letter for letter, stroke for stroke. In other words, not just the words are important to God. The dotting of the "I's" and the crossing of the "T's" are equally important to and inspired by God. Every word, which includes every letter and every stroke of the letter, is God-breathed.

Let's go back to our initial question: What is so significant about Eve's exclusion of the word "free"? God views His Word very seriously, and so should we. Speaking about the book of Revelation, God says, *"If anyone takes words away from this book of prophecy, God will take away from him his share in the tree of life and in the holy city, which are described in this book"* (Revelation 22:19). Every word of God is important to God.

If every word is important to God, then I submit that it should be equally important to us. Satan planted a tiny seed of doubt in Eve's mind. She let herself think about it, and her response to the Devil was tainted. By omitting the word "free," Eve made God appear to be miserly, selfishly holding back something from them. This, in turn, meant that God was actually all about Himself, and He didn't really care about them. The removal of just one word made God into something that He is not.

Even today we must be very careful not to take away from God's Word. When we begin to doubt God's Word — not going to Him for the answers to our questions, and even our doubts — we will find that it is much easier to forget what He really said, and to start to detract from God's Word. Eventually we will disobey God's Word and His will.

Satan wants to deceive your mind and to draw you away from the simplicity that is in Christ. Just as he did with Eve, he will begin by getting you to question God's Word. All he wants you to do is to begin to ask yourself the question, "Did God really say that?" When he is able to get you to question God's Word, his next step is to deny the truth of what God actually said.

Say It Ain't True

"'*You will not surely die,' the serpent said to the woman*" (Gen. 3:4). I can almost hear the serpent's voice dripping with sarcasm. Can't you just see him snort at Eve's answer, roll his eyes as he says, "C'mon, do you really think that you're going to die? You're not going to die! God's holding back on you, and you know it."

I submit for your consideration that when you begin to question God's Word, it becomes much easier to deny God's truth. You see, when you begin to doubt the truth of what God says, it becomes easy for you to decide to do something other than what God says. This is Satan's subtle ploy: to deceive your mind, leading you away from the simplicity that is in Christ. Doubting God's truth, without seeking God and His Word for the answer, inevitably leads to rejecting God's truth.

Look at how Eve responded to Satan's accusation that God wasn't telling the truth: *"God did say, 'You must not eat fruit from the tree that is in the middle of the garden, and you must not touch it, or you will die"* (Gen. 3:3). Did she defend her creator and benefactor? Did she tell Satan he was full of it and to get lost? We can see the deceit at work in her mind. She's allowing herself to continue to think about what Satan is saying. The seed of doubt is becoming bigger, and her thoughts are now pulling her farther away from the actual truth.

Consider what God had actually said: *"You must not eat from the tree of the knowledge of good and evil, for when you eat of it you will surely die"* (Gen. 2:17). You can see Eve's error. When we compare these two verses we find that Eve not only subtracted from God's Word, but she added her own words to God's Word. She added, *"You must not touch it."*

Why was she wrong in adding to what God said? After all, isn't it a good thing to not even touch the forbidden fruit? The bottom line is that when she added to God's Word, Eve did two things. First, she made God out to be less kind and giving. She stopped remembering all that God had lovingly provided for her — she had an entire garden at her disposal. Instead, she set her focus on what God was not allowing her to have. She believed that God was infringing upon her rights; that there was no comprehensible reason why she couldn't eat of that fruit, other than the fact that God was being selfish.

The second thing she did by adding to God's Word was to make God's command a load too heavy to bear. Adding an additional restriction which demanded far too much. You can almost hear her thinking: "How could God possibly expect me to walk through the garden and not think about this particular tree? Doesn't He realize how hard it is to not eat of it?" The truth is God's commands are not a burden to those who belong to Him (1 John 5:3-4). Eve added to God's Word and thus altered God's truth, warping it into something God never intended it to be — all about her.

In Deuteronomy 4:2 God says, *"Do not add to what I command you and do not subtract from it, but keep the commands of the Lord your God."* And in Deuteronomy 12:32 we read, *"See that you do all I command you; do not add to it or take away from it."* The book of Proverbs adds, *"Do not add to His words, or He will rebuke you and prove you a liar"* (Prov. 30:6). God makes it very clear that He takes His Word seriously, and so should we.

When Is A Lie True?

Satan does not want you to live in victory over sin. He does not want you to live a godly life. He is waging an all-out war against you to keep you from letting your light shine in such a way that others will see your good works and give glory to God (Matt. 5:16). To that end, he is attacking your mind with his cunning deceit to keep you from the simplicity that is in Christ. The way he does this is to get you to question God's Word, so that you are open to denying God's truth and vulnerable to accepting his own lie as actual truth.

Satan told Eve, *"God knows that when you eat of it your eyes will be opened, and you will be like God, knowing good and evil"* (Gen. 3:5). Can you recognize Satan's boldfaced lie? When God created man, He said, *"Let us make man in our image, in our likeness...So God created man in His own image, in the image of God He created him"* (Gen. 1:26, 27). Adam and Eve were already made in the image of God and they knew that. Yet Satan got them to doubt that truth, and then to deny that truth and to accept his substituted lie in the place of God's truth. A lie is a lie, it will never be true. But Satan is adept at getting us to believe that his lie is the truth.

Listen carefully. Satan's lie was that they would be like God. This meant far more than simply being created in God's image.

Satan was tempting them to believe that they themselves could be God. Yet in God's Word, Moses declared, *"There is no one like the Lord our God"* (Exod: 8:10). God said of Himself, *"there is no one like me in all the earth"* (Exod. 9:14). Samuel cries out, *"How great you are, O Sovereign Lord! There is no one like you, and there is no God but you"* (2 Sam. 7:22). King David prays, *"There is no one like you, O Lord, and there is no God but you"* (1 Chron. 17:20). And in Isaiah 46:9 God says, *"I am God, and there is no other; I am God, and there is none like me."*

This is the absolute truth that permeates the Scriptures: No one can be like God. Yet, when Satan got man to question God's Word, and then deny God's truth, man was not only open to believing Satan's lie but he received it as truth. Adam and Eve actually believed that God was selfishly holding back on them and that by eating the fruit they would experience full deity for themselves.

Surely You Jest

There is one more thing that Eve did in response to Satan's deception. As we have seen, she first omitted God's Word, then she added to God's Word, and finally, she completely changed God's Word. She said, *"…and you must not touch it, or you will die"* (Gen. 3:3). If you read too quickly, you can miss the significance of what she just said. We need to compare this with what God actually said in Genesis 2:17, *"For when you eat of it you will **surely** die"* (emphasis mine).

God said they would "surely" die. But Eve omitted the word "surely." By that omission she changed God's Word. She moved the penalty of disobedience from the firm and absolute promise that upon disobedience you will surely die, into the realm of mere possibility.

When we try to figure out answers to our doubts without looking to God's Word, we become vulnerable to input from ungodly influences. When we begin to doubt God's Word and deny God's truth — thereby allowing deceitful lies to take place of absolute truth — we will begin to consider our daily actions apart from God's Word. We will no longer see the necessity for God's Word. Satan was able to get Eve to consider the tree apart from what God had said because she allowed her mind to initially doubt and question God's Word. This made her open to rejecting God's truth, which made her completely vulnerable to listening to the Devil's lie in the place of truth.

In the end, Adam and Eve discovered that God's truth is indeed absolute truth.

> *"When the woman saw that the fruit of the tree was good for food and pleasing to the eye, and also desirable for gaining wisdom, she took some and ate it. She also gave some to her husband, who was with her, and he ate it. Then the eyes of both of them were opened, and they realized they were naked; so they sewed fig leaves together and made coverings for themselves" (Gen. 3:6-7).*

On that day, at that very moment, they did surely die — not physically, but they were separated from God.

This is exactly what Satan is trying to accomplish in your life. He wants to get you away from God's truth so that you can consider your life and make your daily decisions apart from God, God's truth, and God's perfect and pleasing will for your life. After all these years, his strategy hasn't changed. All he needs to do is plant a seed of doubt in your mind. If you don't yield your will to God through His Spirit, your mind will take it from there.

Think Before You Act

When you question God's Word, you begin to doubt whether it really is absolute truth. As a result, you begin to focus on yourself and all the perceived "rights" that are being denied you because you are interpreting God's standards as burdensome and unloving. From there, your mind begins to linger on the pleasures that sin can afford and you begin to think about things apart from the absolute truth of God's Word. At this point, it is a very short step toward outright disobedience to your Heavenly Father. All Satan has to do is get you to choose to think about things *apart* from the Word of God. We must continue to learn how vital it is that we consider everything in life in light of God's Word. God's truth must be our guide in every aspect of life.

You must be in the Word of God daily. It is fundamentally imperative that you continuously saturate your mind with God's truth, because *"No lie comes from the truth"* (1 John 2:21). You and I face the same choice daily that Eve did — God's truth or Satan's lie? When you dilute and change God's truth, it is easy for you to reject that truth, believe the lie, and choose to sin.

Satan is not your friend. He does not care about your pleasure or enjoyment. He does not want you to be happy. He wants your destruction. Jesus told Peter, *"Satan [desires] to have you that he may sift you as wheat"* (Luke 22:31 KJV). Peter later recorded, *"Be self-controlled and alert. Your enemy the devil prowls around like a roaring lion looking for someone to devour. Resist him, standing firm in the faith"* (1 Pet. 5:8, 9).

Note that Peter says you are to be "self-controlled." In other words, you are to be in your right mind, thinking properly. Why? Because Satan, your enemy, is on the hunt, looking for someone to devour. When a lioness is on the hunt, she knows that the best target is the weak one. When she comes upon a herd of antelope, she crouches low in the grass and waits, watching to see which one is the weakest — the easiest target. This, Peter says, is what Satan does. He is looking for the Christian who is weak in the faith, the one who isn't hiding God's Word in their heart, focusing all of their thoughts on glorifying God. You should always be in your right mind, thinking properly, and on guard against the attack of the enemy with his deceitful lies.

Favoring the Prepared Mind

Consider this warning from Peter: *"Prepare your minds for action; be self-controlled; set your hope fully on the grace to be given you when Jesus Christ is revealed"* (1 Pet. 1:13). We need to prepare our minds for action! Peter writes the verb "to prepare" in the middle voice, which means it is to your advantage to have your mind prepared for action.

Your mind is the place where your behavior begins, so it benefits you greatly to have a prepared mind. Peter says specifically that you are to prepare your mind for "action." Your mind needs to be prepared for the kind of action we just saw in the life of Eve, because, as Peter warns, our enemy is seeking to devour us. He wants to deceive your mind with his subtle lies. The action you need to prepare your mind for is fighting off Satan's deceitful lies.

Notice that Peter says, in 1 Peter 5:8-9, you are to "be self-controlled" — in your right mind, always thinking properly. Not only are you to be self-controlled, but also "alert." In other words, you are to be awake and watchful, circumspect. Satan's attack can come at any time! And when it does, you are to "resist" him, standing firm in the faith. You are to set yourself against him, in opposition, with both your words and your deeds. You are to "stand firm," solidly and immovably planted in the firm foundation of God's Word. And notice, as you do, that the enemy will flee from you.

Peter goes on to say that you are to stand firm "in the faith." This is done when you *"stand firm then, with the belt of truth buckled around your waist, with the breastplate of righteousness in place"* (Eph. 6:14). Note Paul's use of the word "with." It indicates that you are fully equipped for the battle. Think about that. God is telling us that when we wear the belt of truth we are standing firm in the faith, fully equipped for the battle! And what is truth? God's Word is truth.

Let's put this all together in a way that makes sense. We are to resist the devil. This is done as we stand firm in the faith. How do we stand firm in the faith? By being fully equipped for the battle, which includes wearing the belt of truth — the Word of God. Therefore, saturating your mind with the Scriptures helps you stand firm! Standing firm in the faith begins by being in God's Word daily.

When you know God's truth you will be able to quickly identify Satan's attacks on your mind with his deceitful lies, and immediately say "no" to them. You won't flirt with them; you won't consider them in the slightest. You will promptly dismiss them for what they are — lies intended to destroy your relationship with God and your testimony to the world around you. The command in Scripture is to *"submit yourselves, then, to God. Resist the devil, and he will flee from you"* (Jas. 4:7). Note the order here. You are to first submit yourself to God (yielding control of all your life to Him), and then you are to resist the devil. But how do we resist the devil? Peter said that we resist the devil when we stand firm in the faith (1 Pet. 5:9). We stand firm in the faith when we are daily in God's Word. When we yield control of our life to God and stand firm in the faith, Satan will flee from us!

Have you noticed that our ongoing theme is all about God's Word? There is a reason for that. God's Word reveals God's will. Apart from the truth of the Word of God we have no sure understanding of the will of God. To that end, Satan wants to attack your mind with his deceit so you will not *trust* in God's Word, thereby not *knowing* what God's will is — finally, not *doing* God's will. You are to *"be very careful, then, how you live — not as unwise but as wise, making the most of every opportunity, because the days are evil. Therefore do not be foolish, but understand what the Lord's will is"* (Eph. 5:15-17).

Puzzle Me This

God not only wants you to know His will but to understand it as well. That verb, "to understand," in Ephesians 5:17, gives the idea of collecting together the features of an object and looking at it as a whole. That is the only way you can fully comprehend it. The best example I can give you is a thousand-piece jigsaw puzzle. Have you ever tried to put one of those monstrosities together? You can study the individual pieces to gain an understanding of how the pieces fit together, but until you put each of those pieces where they belong you will not be able to see the whole picture. Think about it this way: If I were to hand you a single piece from that puzzle, would you be able to tell me what the big picture was by looking at that piece? Even if I gave you two, three, or four pieces, you would probably not be able to tell me what the picture is. Simply looking at a couple of those pieces is not going to give you a full comprehension of what the whole picture is. You need to gather together all of the pieces and put them all together.

In the same way, you cannot understand what God's will is unless you gather together all the pieces of Scripture and, through the guidance of the Holy Spirit, put them all together. Paul is saying that the foolish person tries to live his or her life apart from God's will. This is the same foolish person from Matthew 7 who hears God's Word yet chooses to ignore it. This, my friend, is exactly what Satan wants you to do. Your responsibility here is to seek — under the direction of the Holy Spirit — all the pieces of God's will (through a continuous study of God's Word) and put them together so you can comprehend what His total will is. That cannot be done by only listening to Sunday's sermon or going to a Bible study. You need to be in the Word of God every day. You must search the Scriptures daily. God may lead you through a particular message or a Bible study, but it will require your personal attention to His Word. You must search the scriptures. It is a personal action and pursuit.

The Psalmist cried out, *"Send forth your light and your truth, let them guide me; let them bring me to your holy mountain, to the place where you dwell"* (Ps. 43:3). God's light is found in God's Word (Ps. 119:105), and God's truth is found in God's Word (Jn.

17:17). The Word of God is absolute truth that will guide you in how to live a life that glorifies and honors Him.

Apart from the Word of God you have no sure understanding of the purposes God has for your life. Yes, God does have a purpose for you. God knows you. He created you. He understands you. He cares for you and has a good and perfect plan for your life. So how are you doing in your study of the Scriptures? Are you in it every day? Are you faithfully hiding His Word in your heart? Are you digging into the depths of the Word to find the deep and wondrous truths buried there? I love the words of Acts 22:14, *"The God of our fathers has chosen you to know His will."* God wants you to know His will. He also wants you to understand His will. We are commanded, *"Do not be foolish, but understand what the Lord's will is"* (Eph. 5:17). Paul's prayer for the saints at Colossae was that God would fill them *"with the knowledge of His will through all spiritual wisdom and understanding"* (Col. 1:9).

Not only do we need to know God's will and understand what God's will is, we need to be *filled* with the knowledge of God's will. To "fill" literally means to be full to the top so that there is no room for anything else. You must be so filled with the knowledge of God's will that there is no room for even one of Satan's lies to take root. When you are filled with the knowledge of God's will, you will *"[Do] the will of God from your heart"* (Eph. 6:6). And God's will is not a duty, it's a delight. Think about it this way, God is conforming His children to the *"likeness of His Son"* (Romans 8:29). Well, just like Christ, you should be able to truthfully say, *"My food…is to do the will of [God] who sent me and to finish His work"* (John 4:34). Wow! Think about that for a moment. God wants you to be able to say that your food, your nourishment, and the place you draw strength to make it through the day, is in doing God's will. Remember that Romans 12:2 says, *"Do not conform any longer to the pattern of this world, but be transformed by the renewing of your mind. Then you will be able to test and approve what God's will is — His good, pleasing and perfect will."*

Satan does not want you to know what God's will is. When you are ignorant of God's will, you end up making bad decisions. You get involved in sinful activities. You build the wrong kind of spiritual home on shifting sands, so that when the storms of life come raging in on you, the life you have built for yourself will come crashing down all around you. You end up wasting your life instead of investing all that you are in the Kingdom of God.

Draw Your Sword

The only way to counter Satan's attack on your mind is through the Word of God. Paul instructs us to *"Take the helmet of salvation and the sword of the Spirit, which is the Word of God"* (Eph. 6:17). Focus on the fact that you are to "take" the sword. This verb is written in the active voice, imperative mood. If you recall, active voice means you are the one to do the action, no one else can do it for you. And the imperative simply means it is a command. In other words, God commands you to take the sword of the Spirit and use it. No one else can do this for you, and if you don't do this, you are disobeying a direct command of Scripture. It is personal. It requires action.

You may be wondering what the sword of the Spirit is. The word "sword" does not refer to the typical long-blade or broadsword that we usually see in the movies. You know the typical scenes I'm referring to: There is an epic battle and the soldier has pulled his sword out of the sheath at his side and is expertly swinging it around, lopping off heads for a glorious victory. Well, that isn't the sword Paul is talking about. Rather, it actually refers to a small dagger used specifically in close, hand-to-hand combat. This is significant and has powerful meaning. Our enemy, the Devil, sneaks in close — like a lion — for the kill. It is not efficient to make large, broadsword strokes when battling against our enemy. When facing temptation, making general sweeping statements such as, "Well, the Bible says I shouldn't do that," isn't going to win the battle. That is too broad of a stroke and leaves a lot of gaps for the enemy to get into. You need to use the dagger approach. *Where* exactly does it say it? *What* exactly does it say? *Why* exactly shouldn't I do that?

Only the inspired Word of God can show you Satan's lies for what they are. Only the inspired Word of God can enable you to defeat his vicious attacks. You cannot reason with the enemy. You can't even have a conversation with him. Your wisdom is no match. Don't simply believe me on this — look to God's absolute truth. Only God's wisdom, which is revealed in His Word, is victorious over the enemy. Your only defense is the inspired Word of God, which is living, powerful, and sharper than any two-edged sword (Heb. 4:12).

The Gospel of Matthew reveals how Jesus wielded the Sword of Truth:

> *"Then Jesus was led by the Spirit into the desert to be tempted by the devil. After fasting forty days and forty nights, He was hungry. The tempter came to Him and said, 'If you are the Son of God, tell these stones to become bread.' Jesus answered, 'It is written: 'Man does not live on bread alone, but on every word that comes from the mouth of God.' Then the devil took Him to the holy city and had Him stand on the highest point of the temple. 'If you are the Son of God,' he said, 'throw yourself down. For it is written: 'He will command His angels concerning you, and they will lift you up in their hands, so that you will not strike your foot against a stone.' Jesus answered him, 'It is also written: 'Do not put the Lord your God to the test.'" (Matt. 4:1-7).*

Did you notice that while tempting Jesus, Satan actually quoted Scripture? The enemy does indeed know Scripture, and he knows how to use it against us. There are a couple of important things to note here. First, he intentionally quoted only part of the verse and thus misrepresented the text. Second, Satan will never use the Scriptures to lead you *into* God's will but away from it. So how can we defeat that? How can we know whether it's the enemy speaking God's Word to us or the Holy

Spirit? Look at how Jesus responded. He countered Satan's use of the Scripture with other Scripture. He said, *"It is also written."* Jesus' example here shows us the critical importance of always comparing Scripture with Scripture. Never take a verse and just use that one text to support your action or decision. Always, my friend, always compare that verse with the rest of God's Word!

Continuing in Matthew 4:

> *"Again, the devil took Him to a very high mountain and showed Him all the kingdoms of the world and their splendor. 'All this I will give you,' he said, 'if you will bow down and worship me.' Jesus said to him, 'Away from me, Satan! For it is written: 'Worship the Lord your God, and serve Him only."* Then the *devil left Him, and angels came and attended Him"* (Matt. 4:8-11).

It is important for us to notice that Jesus did not use His divine power to defeat Satan. He provided an example for us by using the same weapon that we have available to us today, namely, the Word of God.

Also notice that Satan could not counter the truth of God's Word. Every time Jesus quoted scripture, Satan was finished with that particular temptation. His lies can never stand up against God's absolute truth. We are commanded to *"resist the devil and he will flee from you"* (Jas. 4:7). We resist him the same way Jesus did, with Scripture. If you are going to defeat Satan's attacks on your mind with his deceitful lies you must depend upon the Word of God.

Catching the Counterfeit

To recognize whether something is a lie of Satan, you need to know the truth of God. Allow me to illustrate. Many, many moons ago I tried my hand at being a bank teller. Let's just say that math and I are not good friends and this job proved it in spades. Anyway, while I was being trained for the position, my trainer slid two $5 bills across the table in front of me. "You have ten seconds to identify the counterfeit bill," she said and began her stopwatch. Thinking I would impress her, I picked up one of the bills, held it up to the light, felt it, sniffed it, crinkled it, then unwrinkled it, did everything I could to it; I then repeated the process with the other bill. At the end of the allotted time I was nowhere closer to my objective than when I had started. "Do you want to know how to identify a counterfeit?" she asked me (what was I going to do, say "no ma'am"?). Placing her finger on one of the bills, she pulled it back toward her, and then pushed the remaining bill closer to me. "To immediately identify a counterfeit bill," she said, "become intimately familiar with the real thing." Wow, talk about a great lesson — and I'm not talking about banking here!

My days as a bank teller didn't last very long, but that lesson has stuck with me for life. To recognize whether something is a lie of Satan, become intimately familiar with the real thing — God's truth. There is absolutely no reason today why any person reading this book should be ignorant of the Scriptures. We have been blessed to have the Bible available to us in many different translations. What's more, we have the Holy Spirit dwelling within us to teach us the truths of the Word. Remember Jesus' promise that the Holy Spirit *"will guide you into all truth"* (John 16:13), and His promise that the Spirit will remind you of what God says in His Word (John 14:26). In other words, as you study Scripture, the Holy Spirit will help you understand God's Word and will guide you in how to apply it to your life.

When you are exposed to one of Satan's lies, the Holy Spirit will remind you of what God's truth says. Yet in order for that to happen, you must *invest* your time in reading and studying the Bible. I want you to realize that there is a difference between spending and investing. When you spend, you are giving up what you have for some perceived immediate benefit or pleasure that is short-lived — it doesn't last. When you invest, you are giving up something now to get something much bigger in the future. This is why it is so important that you must *invest* your time in reading and studying the Bible. You may be giving up time now that could've been used for other things, but the time invested now in studying God's Word will reap huge benefits later when faced with trials and temptations.

Consider this:

> *"If any man builds on this foundation using gold, silver, costly stones, wood, hay or straw, his work will be shown for what it is, because the Day will bring it to light. It will be revealed with fire, and the fire will test the quality of each man's work. If what he has built survives, he will receive his reward. If it is burned up, he will suffer loss; he himself will be saved, but only as one escaping through the flames" (1 Corinthians 3:12-15).*

Paul points out in this passage that every believer is building his or her spiritual house on the same foundation — Jesus Christ. But God allows you to build on top of that foundation however you please. Every action, every choice, every word spoken is a piece of the godly life you are building. When you are *spending* your time on these things, it's like building with wood, hay or straw — it's not going to last, because your motivations are for selfish gain. But when you *invest* your time for God you are building with gold, silver, and costly stones. Your heart's motivation is to bring honor and glory to God, regardless of what you may or may not get out of it.

In order to recognize whether something is a lie of Satan, you need to know the truth of God. This means you must first invest time in getting to know God's Word. Second, you must memorize God's Word. When Jesus was tempted in the wilderness, He didn't carry a copy of the Scriptures and a Bible concordance under His arm. Then, when Satan threw a temptation at Him, Jesus didn't hold up a finger and say, "Wait a minute while I look that up," or, "Let me talk with the pastor about this one." Jesus relied on the Spirit to remind Him of what he had read, studied, and learned. Then, from both memory and being guided by the Holy Spirit, He quoted Scripture to silence the lies of Satan and thwart his attacks. In short, He used the sword of the Spirit, which is the Word of God.

Be a Treasure Hunter

David cries out, "*I have hidden your word in my heart that I might not sin against you*" (Ps. 119:11). How well do you know the Scriptures? Notice that David didn't say, "I have read your word," or even, "I have studied your word." He said, "*I have hidden your word in my heart.*" The verb, "to hide," means "to store up as a treasure." Do you see God's Word as "treasure"? For the lack of a better illustration, think of a pirate. When he plunders and gets his treasures, he finds a secret spot and hides it. Is he content with those few items? Of course not. He goes out and looks for more to add to his booty. That's the idea of this verb "to hide." Don't rely only on the verses you memorized as a child for Sunday School. Be continuously in God's Word. Memorize it. Store it up in your heart. Add more and more to what you already have.

Let's say I go to the hardware store and spend over an hour looking at all the tools. I look at some really great hammers, saws, drills, tape measurers, levels, and screwdrivers. I look at them and study their details. I handle them and gain an understanding of what they do and how they work. But I never buy them. Then I go home and begin a major project that I've been putting off. It's time to begin, but I have no tools. They're still at the hardware store. I did not invest in them to make them mine. I won't be able to complete my project in a timely, accurate, and proper way because I don't have the tools and equipment that I need.

So it is with our battle against Satan. If you just come to church on Sunday and listen to the message; if you just occasionally open your Bible and read it, gaining a head knowledge of what the text is about, then you have not adequately prepared yourself for the enemy's attack on your mind. You have not given the Holy Spirit the proper tools required to provide you with a proper defense. One ministry of the Spirit is to remind you of what God has said. He cannot do that if you have not hidden God's Word in your heart. When you face temptation, the Holy Spirit brings back to your mind Biblical truths that you have read, studied, meditated upon, memorized, and stored up in your heart. But if you do not read, study, and memorize God's Word, with an understanding of how it applies to your life, then when the enemy's attack comes, you will not able to experience this work of the Holy Spirit.

To recognize whether something is a lie of Satan, you must know the truth of God. This comes as you know God's Word, by meditating on it and memorizing His truth. God instructed Joshua to *"not let this Book of the Law depart from your mouth; meditate on it day and night, so that you may be careful to do everything written in it. Then you will be prosperous and successful"* (Josh. 1:8).

David says the blessed man's delight *"is in the law of the LORD, and on His law he meditates day and night"* (Ps. 1:2). He later declares, *"I will meditate on all your works and consider all your mighty deeds"* (Ps. 77:12). He prays, *"Let me understand the teaching of your precepts; then I will meditate on your wonders"* (Ps. 119:27). Notice the process here. First you read God's Word, then you seek to understand what you have read (study), and then you meditate on the truth and principles God has revealed to you. You need to claim, along with David, *"I meditate on your precepts and consider your ways"* (Ps. 119:15). Can you honestly say *"Oh, how I love your law! I meditate on it all day long"* (Ps. 119:97)? It is God's purpose that when you meditate on His Word you will gain more insight than all your teachers (Ps. 119:99).

Don't just put God's Word in your mouth and chew it for a moment, then spit it back out — never swallowing it. If you ate all your meals like that, you would become weak and sickly. It's the same with your spiritual life and the Scriptures. You are to chew it and swallow it and bring it back up again on a regular basis to chew on it some more, thinking about it, and then applying it to your life. Not once, not twice, but continuously every day.

God says that His Word *"is [to be] in your mouth and in your heart so you may obey it"* (Deut. 30:14). Jeremiah said, *"When your words came, I ate them; they were my joy and my heart's delight"* (Jer. 15:16). Oh, my friend, I hope you sincerely delight in it, not just reading it because you should, but taking time to actually feed on God's truth. I hope you are learning to read it, think about it, memorize it, and meditate on it regularly.

"Finally, brothers, whatever is true, whatever is noble, whatever is right, whatever is pure, whatever is lovely, whatever is admirable — if anything is excellent or praiseworthy — think about such things"
Philippians 4:8

~ Fourteen ~
Think on These Things

Paul writes *"Finally, brothers, whatever is true, whatever is noble, whatever is right, whatever is pure, whatever is lovely, whatever is admirable — if anything is excellent or praiseworthy — think about such things"* (Phil. 4:8). Focus your attention on the last four words of this verse. To "think about such things," is to thoroughly occupy your mind with these six things. In other words, you should be thinking so much about these things that there is no room for any sinful thought to find entrance or to take root.

I can just hear someone raise the question, "Are you saying that if I fill my mind with these things, I won't ever think a sinful thought again?" No. What I am saying is this: When you faithfully check every thought against the grid of these six things, sinful thoughts will have no place to take up occupancy in your mind. You will not even think about how to gratify the desires of the flesh. When a thought enters your mind that doesn't match up with any of these six things, you will refuse to allow that thought to have any place in your thinking process. In fact, it may not even take a conscious effort to cast it out. The sinful thought will just fall away or be cast out because there is no place for it to fit.

My friend, *every* thought should be filtered through the grid of Philippians 4:8. Again I can hear someone exclaim, "Wait a minute Steve. *Every* thought? C'mon, that's impossible! I think hundreds, if not thousands, of thoughts every day, and you expect me to stop to consider every one of those thoughts?" Let me simply say this, God's command is clear in Philippians 4:8. *"Think on these things."* This isn't my suggestion here; it is God's command. You are to thoroughly occupy your mind with these things so that there is no room for a sinful thought to settle in. Let me encourage you that God will never command you to do something that is impossible to do. In fact, right after writing Philippians 4:8, Paul goes on to declare, *"I can do everything through Him who gives me strength"* (Phil. 4:13). God has given us His Spirit to live in us and be our life and our strength. God has given us all we need to accomplish what He commands.

In 2 Corinthians 10:5 we are commanded to *"Take captive every thought to make it obedient to Christ."* Wow! That is powerful. Let's break this down so we can better understand what God is commanding us to do.

First, you are to "take captive" every thought. This is written in the present tense, active voice. Present tense means that this action is something that is to be done non-stop, always in the present or real time. You are never to stop or take a break from taking every thought captive. The active voice means you are the one responsible for this action. No one else can take your thoughts captive and make them obedient to Christ. It is personal. If it's going to be done, you are the one who must do it.

Now think on the word "captive." The root word means to lead captive as a prisoner of war at the point of a sword. The sword you are to use to take your thoughts captive is the Word of God. *"For the Word of God is living and active. Sharper than any double-edged sword, it penetrates even to dividing soul and spirit, joints and marrow; it judges the thoughts and attitudes of the heart"* (Heb. 4:12). The only thing that can take your sinful thoughts into captivity is Scripture.

Remember what we discovered in Ephesians 6:17. We are to take the sword of the Spirit, which is the Word of God. This sword is that short dagger that is used in close, hand-to-hand combat. This sword of the Spirit refers to specific verses and passages of Scripture that the Holy Spirit uses to address specific temptations and issues in your life. The only way to take your sinful thoughts captive is by using the Word of God. You must attack each thought with something that is far greater than that thought. What is greater than a sinful thought of anger, lust, covetousness, pride, or worry? The Word of God! Faith in God and His Word is more powerful than any fiery dart of the enemy that may come flying at you. Through the use of God's Word — specific Scripture that you have read, studied, memorized, and meditated upon — you can take every thought captive. Your mind is the battlefield where Satan engages you to gain access to your life. You must set up a guard that stands ready to take every thought captive as a prisoner of war.

Look again at 2 Corinthians 10:5, *"Take captive every thought to make it obedient to Christ."* What is it you are to take captive? Not just some of your thoughts, not even most of your thoughts. You are responsible to take captive *every* thought, and make it follow God's commands. It doesn't matter where the thought originated from, whether from the television, the radio, a book, a movie, another person, or even an original thought of your own, you must take every thought captive to the obedience of Christ.

I challenge you to memorize Philippians 4:8 and 2 Corinthians 10:5, and then discipline yourself to run every single thought you think past the following six questions. As you do, evaluate each thought and take captive those that do not bring glory to God, casting them out.

Is it True?
The first question to ask yourself is this: Is this thought based on things that are true? The word "true" refers to that which conforms to reality or fact. It is real and genuine. It is based upon, and is consistent with, God's perfect standard. Where will you find this truth? David cried out to God, *"O Lord God, you are God! Your words are true"* (2 Sam. 7:28 ESV). The

Word of God is absolute truth (Jn. 17:17). God's Word is real, genuine, and conforms to reality and fact. There is no deceit in God's Word. Paul is telling us in Philippians 4:8 that our minds should be so filled with God's truth that there is no room for Satan's lies to take root. Remember the illustration of a bank teller identifying a counterfeit bill. You should be so familiar with God's truth that you can instantly identify Satan's deceitful lies no matter how cunning they may be. Every thought you think should be evaluated according to these questions: Is this thought based on God's truth? Is it based on reality? Does it conform to God's perfect standards? If what you are thinking is not true according to God's Word, then don't think about it.

You cannot get rid of sinful thoughts simply by *trying not to think* them. If I told you, "Whatever you do, don't think about pink flowers," you know what you would start to think about? Pink flowers! For some reason, when we determine that we're not going to think about something, that is when we think about it even more. You cannot overcome sinful thoughts simply by choosing not to think about them. You need to focus upon God's truth, and keep focusing on the truth, until the sinful thoughts are drowned out and replaced by God's truth.

You should *"Let the peace of Christ rule in your hearts"* (Col. 3:15). This happens as you *"Let the word of Christ dwell in you richly"* (Col. 3:16). The end result is that *"Whatever you do, whether in word or deed, [it will all be done] in the name of the Lord Jesus"* (Col. 3:17). When you choose to think only those thoughts that are true — that agree with the Word of God — then you will know *"the peace of God, which transcends all your understanding,"* and it *"will guard your hearts and your minds in Christ Jesus"* (Phil. 4:7). This is crucial. Remember, you are to *"above all else guard your heart"* (Prov. 4:23). Paul declares that the peace of God is what will guard your heart and mind. To have God's peace, you must let God's Word *dwell in you richly*!

Philippians 4:8 says you are to think (thoroughly occupy your mind) on things that are true. Evaluate each thought and take captive those that are not true, real, genuine, or consistent with God's perfect standard. Cast them out.

Is it Noble?

The second thing you should thoroughly occupy your mind with is things that are *"noble"* (Phil. 4:8). The word "noble" carries the idea of things that are honorable or worthy of respect. Do you think thoughts that are respectable? If every one of your thoughts were flashed up on a screen for others to see, would they respect you? You are to *"make it your ambition to lead a quiet life, to mind your own business and to work with your hands...so that your daily life may win the respect of outsiders"* (1 Thess. 4:11, 12). The fact is, we are to lead lives that are worthy of respect (Titus 2:2). Your thoughts should be noble thoughts, thoughts that are honorable and would command respect from others if they knew them. The fact is, they will know them because what you think becomes what you do. Even more important is that God already knows your thoughts, and we should desire to please Him with thoughts that are honorable and worthy of respect.

Philippians 4:8 says you are to think (thoroughly occupy your mind) on things that are noble. Evaluate your thoughts and take captive those that are unworthy of respect and cast them out.

Is it Right?

You should thoroughly occupy your mind with things that are true, things that are worthy of respect (noble), and things that are *"right"* (Phil. 4:8). The word "right" refers to being in total conformity to God's will. In other words, things on which God would say, "Yes, that's a right thought!" God instructed Cain to do what is right (Gen. 4:7). God told the children of Israel to *"Listen carefully to the voice of the LORD your God and do what is right in His eyes...pay attention to His commands and keep all His decrees"* (Exod. 15:26; cp. Deut. 6:18). God promises that *"If you do whatever I command you and walk in my ways and do what is right in my eyes by keeping my statutes and commands, as David my servant did, I will be with you"* (1 Kings 11:38). You will choose to walk in God's way and do what is right when you occupy your thoughts with those things found in God's Word, saturating your mind with His truth and determining to walk in obedience to His statutes and commands.

Psalm 25:9 says that God *"guides the humble in what is right and teaches them His way."* It is through the Scriptures that we learn to think right thoughts and do right things. God has given us His Word to guide us in thinking and doing what is right and just and fair (Prov. 1:3).

Philippians 4:8 says you are to think (thoroughly occupy your mind) on things that are right. Evaluate your thoughts. Does God look with approval on this thought? If the answer is no, then you must take that thought captive and make it obedient to Christ (2 Cor. 10:5).

Is it Pure?

According to Philippians 4:8, we should thoroughly occupy our minds with things that are true, worthy of respect (noble), in conformity to God's will (right), and *"pure."* Purity refers to things not contaminated by anything evil. In other words there is no hint of sin to it. It's even purer than Ivory Soap! Psalm 24:3-4 asks the question, *"Who may ascend the hill of the Lord? Who may stand in His holy place? He who has clean hands and a pure heart."*

The Psalmist asks the question, *"How can a young man keep his way pure? By living according to your Word"* (Ps. 119:9). Notice that the question is regarding how to *keep* your way pure. That verb is written in the imperfect tense, meaning it is a process that is ongoing. Pure living is a daily undertaking. In order for you to keep your way pure you must have pure thoughts. Your thoughts must be free from sinful contamination, and it is the Word of God that is going to help you with that.

The reason it is important that you have pure thoughts is because *"The Lord detests the thoughts of the wicked, but those of the pure are pleasing to Him"* (Prov. 15:26). When your thoughts are pleasing to God, your actions will be as well. Your cry should be, *"Create in me a pure heart, O God, and renew a steadfast spirit within me"* (Ps. 51:10).

Philippians 4:8 says you are to think (thoroughly occupy your mind) on things that are right. As you evaluate your thoughts, take thoughts that are impure and tainted by sin captive and make them obedient to Christ. Choose to occupy the thoughts of your mind with that which is clean, modest, and faultless.

Is it Lovely?

Again, according to Philippians 4:8, you are to thoroughly occupy your mind with things that are true, worthy of respect (noble), in conformity to God's will (right), pure (not contaminated by sin), and also *"lovely."* The word "lovely" refers to things that are pleasing, but not pleasing to just anyone. After all, it doesn't really matter what is pleasing to me or to you if it is not pleasing to God. If you are going to live a life that pleases God, it makes sense to find out what pleases Him.

In fact, Scripture commands us to *"find out what pleases the Lord"* (Eph. 5:10). We are told to *"live in order to please God"* (1 Thess. 4:1). We should be able to say as Christ did, *"I always do what pleases the Father"* (John 8:29). We are to *"obey His commands and do what pleases Him"* (1 John 3:22). I submit that doing things that please Him begins by thinking thoughts that please Him. Offering your body to God as a living sacrifice is pleasing to Him (Rom. 12:1), which comes as you are transformed by the renewing of your mind (Rom. 12:2). Living a life of righteousness, peace, and joy in the Holy Spirit is pleasing to God (Rom. 14:17-18), which is a direct result of filling your mind with the knowledge and understanding of His Word. Praying from a pure heart pleases Him (Prov. 15:8), and can only come as your thoughts are pure. Living a peaceful and quiet life in all godliness and holiness is good and pleases God (1 Tim. 2:2-3), which will happen only as your mind is focused on knowing

God's will and living it out daily. Ecclesiastes 2:26 tells us that *"to the man who pleases Him, God gives wisdom, knowledge and happiness."*

In order to please God in everything you say and do, you must first please Him in every thought you think. Choose to occupy your mind with thoughts that are acceptable and pleasing to God. Evaluate each thought and take captive those that are not lovely and pleasing to God, and put them to death.

Is it Admirable?

Paul exhorts us in Philippians 4:8 to thoroughly occupy our minds with things that are true, worthy of respect (noble), in conformity to God's will (right), without a hint of sin to it (pure), well-pleasing to God (lovely), and also *"admirable."* The word "admirable" refers to that which *brings* glory and honor to God. The King James Version uses the words "of good report," which refer to sounding well and being well thought out. If every one of your thoughts became spoken word, they should all sound well to those listening. Remember, what others think of us isn't what matters. God does hear your thoughts, every one of them. Do they sound well to Him?

Your thoughts, especially your thoughts, should bring honor and glory to God. Why? Because what you think becomes what you do, and if your life is going to glorify God, your thoughts must glorify Him. Paul says, *"For you were once darkness, but now you are light in the Lord. Live as children of light (for the fruit of the light consists in all goodness, righteousness and truth)"* (Eph. 5:8-9). When you live as children of light you are letting *"your light shine before men, that they may see your good deeds and praise your Father in heaven"* (Matt. 5:16). The fruit of a life lived in dependency on God is admirable. This is what it means to clothe yourself with the Lord Jesus Christ (Rom 13:14). God's command to the believer is to *"Live such good lives among the pagans that, though they accuse you of doing wrong, they may see your good deeds and glorify God"* (1 Pet. 2:12).

I encourage and urge you to so thoroughly occupy your mind with things that honor and glorify God that your life consistently glorifies Him and causes others to honor Him as well. Philippians 4:8 says you are to think (thoroughly occupy your mind) on things that are admirable. As you evaluate your thoughts, take those thoughts that don't sound well to God — those that do not glorify Him — captive and make them obedient to Christ.

Choose to occupy the thoughts of your mind with that which is true, noble, right, pure, lovely, and admirable. Occupy your mind with thoughts that glorify God!

*"Prepare your minds for action; be self-controlled;
set your hope fully on the grace to be given you when
Jesus Christ is revealed"*
1 Peter 1:13

~ Fifteen ~
The Review

Let's review where we've been. Your mind plays a crucial role in living a life that glorifies God. Remember, if you are going to glorify God in your everyday living, you must first glorify Him in your every-moment thinking. We are told that when we live by the Spirit we will not gratify the desires of the flesh (Gal. 5:16). In fact, we should not even *think* about how to gratify the desires of the flesh (Rom. 13:14), because what we think becomes what we do (Prov. 23:7 KJV).

You have been crucified with Christ. The old nature is dead and gone. You now have a new and holy nature within you that is incapable of sinning. The power of the Holy Spirit lives in you. Yet Paul said that in us, that is, *in our flesh*, dwells no good thing (Rom. 7:18); and that the flesh and the new nature are in constant conflict with each other (Gal. 5:17). The way to victory is to present your body to God every day as a living or continual sacrifice (Rom. 12:1).

A spiritual metamorphosis should be happening in your life, taking that which is on the inside — your new nature — and living it out so that others can see it. This is accomplished as you renovate your thinking — gutting out the old way of thinking (How can I please myself?) and replacing it with a new way of thinking (How can I please God?).

When your mind is focused on how to please self, your actions will be self-centered, resulting in a life that does not glorify God. This is why I keep drilling home the point that if God is to be glorified in your daily life He must first be glorified in your thought life. This can only happen as you saturate your mind with absolute truth (John 17:17). The Word of God is the tool the Holy Spirit uses to renovate your mind.

As Christians, we are to no longer live (to conduct your life after a certain manner) as the unsaved do (Eph. 4:17-24). Maybe you lived like that at one point in your Christian life, but now you know God's truth and that knowledge impacts your life. So be a doer of God's truth (Jas. 1:22). Be a wise builder who not only hears God's Word but also does what it says (Matt. 7:24-27). This requires a constant conscious decision to do what God says you ought to do. And what you use to make these conscious decisions is your mind!

You are to daily put on the new self (Eph. 4:24). Your external actions should reveal the new nature that is within you (this is the transformation Paul speaks of in Rom. 12:2). To put on the new self means to clothe yourself with the new nature — your inner being which has been strengthened through God's Spirit (Eph. 3:16). When you clothe yourself, you are presenting others with that which is pleasing to look at (the nature of God).

Satan is waging an all-out war against the Christian, and the greatest weapon in his arsenal is deception. Satan wants you to be deceived. He wants to draw your attention and focus away from God's truth, so that you will focus on your life, and make your daily decisions, apart from God and His good, perfect, and pleasing will for your life. This is why it is vital that you consider everything in life in the light of God's truth found in God's Word. The Scriptures must be your guide in every aspect of life.

When you are in the Word of God, you will know God's truth. When you know God's truth, you will be able to recognize

Satan's deceptive lies because no lie will ever come from God's truth (1 John 2:21). Eve had been faced with a choice — God's truth or Satan's lie. Because she chose to doubt, water down, and change God's truth, it became easy for her to reject that truth and believe the lie Satan was feeding her. In allowing her mind to turn away from the truth and focus on that which was not true, her actions followed and she sinned.

You are to stand firm in the faith, wearing the belt of truth (Eph. 6:14). God's Word is truth (John 17:17). Standing firm in the faith begins with being in the Word of God every day, saturating your mind with God's absolute truth. Then you are able to solidly stand and say "no" to the enemy.

When you submit yourself to God you will be able to resist the devil, and God promises that the enemy will flee from you (Jas. 4:7). Note the order of events in that verse. First, submit yourself to God, and *then* resist the devil. "To submit" carries the idea of arranging yourself under another, subjecting yourself to obeying someone else, yielding yourself to their complete control.

Submitting to God begins with your mind. There needs to be a conscious decision daily — and even moment by moment — to submit to God's truth. The fact is, *"The sinful mind is hostile to God. It does not submit to God's law, nor can it do so"* (Rom. 8:7). If we are not on our guard constantly, the sinful desires of our flesh will try to influence us to make the choice to yield to our flesh. *"Since you died with Christ to the basic principles of this world, why, as though you still belonged to it, do you submit to its rules?"* (Col. 2:20).

I've said this before: Satan is not your friend. He is on the hunt. He wants to devour you (1 Pet. 5:8-9). Because of this, God commands you to be self-controlled (sober-minded). You should be in your right mind, always thinking properly, on guard against the attack of Satan on your mind with his deceitful lies. The Word of God, through the counsel of the Holy Spirit, is going to help you think properly. The Scriptures are *your* greatest weapon.

Ready, Set, ACTION!

Peter warns, *"Prepare your minds for action; be self-controlled; set your hope fully on the grace to be given you when Jesus Christ is revealed"* (1 Pet. 1:13). Note the command to *"prepare your mind for action."* Focus your attention on the word "prepare." The one who is prepared knows something is coming; they know that something is going to be required of them. They are getting ready for it. The word "action" refers to something that you are *doing*, a specific activity with a definite purpose. You are to specifically prepare your mind.

In the King James Version, it is rendered *"gird up the loins of your mind."* The word "loins" refers to the place where the power to procreate lies. Follow along here because this is powerful stuff. By using the words "loins of your mind," Peter is declaring that your mind is the place where your actions begin. You need to get your thinking in order, otherwise your actions won't line up with God's principles found within God's truth. You are to prepare your mind for action. So exactly what action does your mind need to be prepared for? You need to be prepared for fighting off Satan's attack on your mind with his lies, as well as daily living a life that fully glorifies God.

What are you doing to prepare your mind for action? Where does the Bible fit into your daily schedule? Assuming you are reading the Scriptures and walking with God every day, what then? What are you allowing yourself to watch on television or in the movies? What type of music do you choose to listen to? What types of books, magazines, or RSS feeds are you choosing to read? Do you realize that the influence of those things can either encourage or circumvent your walk with God?

Not only are you to be self-controlled (in your right mind, thinking properly), but also you are to be *"alert"* (1 Pet. 5:8). You are to be spiritually awake and watchful because Satan's attack can come at any time. And when it does, resist him *as you yield to God*. Take a firm stand against him. Set yourself in opposition to him in both words and deeds, under the control of God's Spirit. You are to stand firm, solid and immovable, planted firmly in faith in the absolute truth of God's Word.

The Perfect Law

We are what we think. We have firmly established that we are created for the purpose of glorifying God in our daily lives. We have built this study upon the foundational principle that if we are going to glorify God in our everyday living, He must first be glorified in our every-moment thinking. To do that, we need to renovate our minds. This can only be done through God's absolute truth found in God's Word.

David writes in Psalm 19:7 that *"The law of the Lord is perfect."* What is "the law of the Lord?" Specifically, it is God's commands and instructions which reveal His heart and desire for our good, and show us how to live. The law of the Lord tells us what to do and what not to do in order to please Him. And where do we find the law of the Lord? In God's Word! David declares that God's law is *"perfect."* It is complete, whole, entire, and lacking in nothing. Think about that for a moment. God's Word is complete; it leaves absolutely no gaps!

David then says, *"The statutes of the Lord are trustworthy"* (Ps. 19:7). "Statutes" are rules and guidelines that provide the principles of life. And where do we find the statutes of the Lord? In God's Word. God's statutes, His rules and guidelines for life, are "trustworthy." They are always right. They will never lead you astray or take you down the wrong path.

Next, David says, *"The precepts of the Lord are right"* (Ps. 19:8). A precept is a code of conduct or ethics. And where do we find the precepts of the Lord? In God's Word. David is saying that God's codes of ethics are right. They are empty of any wrong or error. In other words, God has a code of conduct for the

Christian which He reveals in His Word. God's code is pure, it is right; follow it faithfully and you won't do wrong.

Then David says, *"The commands of the Lord are radiant"* (Ps 19:8). The word "commands" literally translates into "words of wisdom." Who has words of wisdom? The question is asked in Job, *"Where can wisdom be found? Where does understanding dwell?"* (Job 28:12). The answer is, *"To God belong wisdom and power; counsel and understanding are His"* (Job 12:13). *"His wisdom is profound, His power is vast"* (Job 9:4). And where will we find God's words of wisdom? In God's Word. Solomon said, *"The LORD gives wisdom, and from His mouth come knowledge and understanding"* (Prov. 2:6). God promises that through His Word, *"[He guides] you in the way of wisdom and [leads] you along straight paths"* (Prov. 4:11). David declared that God's words of wisdom are radiant; they enlighten the eyes. In other words, God's wisdom gives light to help you see the way you should go, it illuminates your path. Think about this. Those words of wisdom are found in the Scriptures, which are *"a lamp to my feet and a light for my path"* (Psa. 119:105). In God alone *"are hidden all the treasures of wisdom and knowledge"* (Col. 2:3), which He has chosen to reveal to us in His Word.

Next, David says, *"The fear of the Lord is pure"* (Ps. 19:9). To fear God means to respect and reverence Him. How do we gain that reverence and respect? By knowing who He is. How do we discover who God is? By studying His Word. David is saying that the Word of God teaches us to hold the God of the Word in high respect and reverence. Furthermore, that fear is pure. In other words, it keeps us morally and spiritually clean before God.

Then David says, *"The ordinances of the Lord are sure and altogether righteous"* (Ps. 19:9). The word "ordinances" refers to legal judgments and decisions made by a judge. God Himself is the Judge of all the earth (Gen. 18:25; cp. Ps. 50:6). He is a righteous judge (Ps. 7:11) who will judge all people righteously and with equity (Jer. 11:20; cp. Ps. 96:10; Isa. 33:22). David is saying that the Word of God teaches us that God is a holy judge, and that all of His judgments are *"sure and altogether righteous."* In other words, they are firm, reliable, and completely just and right.

Think about what we just discovered. God's Word gives you instructions on how to live, rules and guidelines on the principles of life, a code of conduct and ethics, words of wisdom, and an understanding of the fear of the Lord. God's Word is complete, whole, entire, lacking in nothing, trustworthy, always right, it will never take you down the wrong path because it provides a light on your path, it enables you to stay morally and spiritually pure, it is firm, reliable, completely just and right, and it is the final authority in your life!

Do you truly want God to be glorified in your daily life? Sure, you know that you should be glorifying Him, but do you truly want that to be true of your life? For that to happen, God must first be glorified in your thought life. To glorify God in your thoughts you should be consistently filling your mind with His Word and an understanding of His will.

In Conclusion

I know I've brought this verse up often in this book, but let me remind you again of what Paul says in Romans 13:14. *"Clothe yourselves with the Lord Jesus Christ, and do not think about how to gratify the desires of the flesh."* Do not allow even one single, stray thought on how to please the sinful desires of your flesh to take root in your mind. It is essential that everything that goes on in your mind be disciplined toward the goal of bringing honor and glory to God.

Jesus put it this way, *"Love the Lord your God with all your heart and with all your soul and with all your strength and with all your mind"* (Luke 10:27). All of your mind is to be dedicated to loving God. If you are going to love God with all your life, you must first love Him with your entire mind. When you change your thinking to Biblical thinking, the way you live will change to godly living. To live the way God wants you to live, you must think the way God wants you to think.

If you allow yourself to think wrong thoughts, those thoughts will eventually produce wrong actions. It has been my prayer that through this book you will truly begin to understand that you cannot change your life simply by changing your behavior. Dealing with wrong behavior will not change the way you live. You must change your way of thinking if you are going to change your way of living. When your thinking is lined up with God's Word, the enemy will find no entrance into your life. He will come at you, bombarding you with his lies and deceit, trying to penetrate your mind, because that is how he gets leverage and power in a person's life. But when your mind is anchored in God's Word, allowing God's truth to permeate your thinking, you are safe and secure. Listen to God's promise: *"You will keep in perfect peace him whose mind is steadfast, because he trusts in you"* (Isa. 26:3). That "peace" is a peace *"which transcends all understanding, (it) will guard your hearts and your minds in Christ Jesus"* (Phil. 4:7).

Throughout this study I have determined to drive home the point that in order to glorify God in your everyday living He must first be glorified in your every-moment thinking. I've encouraged you to renew your mind, choosing to be in God's Word daily. You see, it is the Word of God, through the power of the Holy Spirit, that washes and cleanses your thought life (Eph. 5:26; cp Titus 3:5-6). We need to seek God's face and ask Him daily to teach us His ways and show us His paths — and then choose to walk in them. God has promised that *"Whether you turn to the right or to the left, your ears will hear a voice behind you, saying, 'This is the way; walk in it'"* (Isa. 30:21).

It is important to remember that unless you change your *way* of thinking, Satan will continue to have access into your life. Before becoming a Christian, Satan owned you and he infiltrated your mind and thinking, filling your mind with land-mines meant to produce destruction in your life. Upon receiving Christ as your Savior, that old nature was crucified and is now dead and gone, but those land-mines may still be there. That old way of thinking still needs to be broken down and replaced with a renewed mind, a new way of thinking, so that you no longer allow access to the devil in your life.

The first thought isn't where sin is, but the subsequent thoughts are those that can get you into trouble and lead you to making sinful choices. When the enemy throws a sinful thought at you and you give in, continuing to dwell on it, it will lead you into sin. However, if at the very moment the impure thought enters your mind, you submit yourself to God, taking that thought captive and resisting the devil, he *will* flee from you (Jas. 4:7).

When you take responsibility for your thoughts, submitting to the work of the Spirit in you, and filling your mind with the truth of God's Word — you will be able to recognize if a thought is wrong and with the power of the Sword of the Spirit, you can tell it to leave. Take every thought captive, my friend, and make it obedient to Christ, bringing glory to God in your thoughts, motives, words, and actions. May your everyday living and your every-moment thinking be pleasing and glorifying to God.

ABOUT THE AUTHOR

Steve Etner is founder and CEO of Renewed Minds Ministries. Having attended Cedarville University and served in the pastorate for 12 years. He is now a speaker and Bible teacher, equipping Christians with the tools necessary to grow in their relationship with God.

His passion is to help others understand the Bible and learn how to apply it to their everyday living. He and his wife, Heather, live in Osceola, Indiana and counsel couples through the Biblical Counseling Center at their church. On the side, Steve helps design web sites as well.

Contact Steve
If you wish to contact Steve or inquire about his availability as a speaker, workshop leader or counselor, you can email him at steve@extrememindmakeover.org.

Who or what is Overboard Books?

Overboard Books publishes quality books that are designed to assist in getting Christians overboard — out of the boat. It's the publishing arm of Overboard Ministries, whose mission is based on Matthew 14. In that chapter we find the familiar story of Jesus walking on water while His disciples were in a boat. It was the middle of the night, the water was choppy and Jesus freaked out His followers who thought He was a ghost. When they realized it was Him, Peter asked to come out to Him on the water, and he actually walked on top of the water like Jesus.

But what truly captivates me is the thought of the other eleven disciples who remained in the boat. I've often wondered how many of them questioned that move in the years to come? How many of them wished they hadn't stayed in the boat but had instead gone overboard with Peter? Overboard Ministries aims to help Christians get out of the boat and live life for Christ out on the water where He is building His Kingdom. We hope and pray that each book published by Overboard Ministries will stir believers to jump overboard and live life all-out for God, full of joy, and free from the regret of "I wish I had…"

What we do
Overboard Books is the publishing arm of Overboard Ministries. Overboard Ministries emerged in the summer of 2010 as an umbrella ministry for several concepts my wife and I were developing. One of those concepts was a book ministry that would help other Christian authors get published. I experienced a lot of frustration while passing my first manuscript around. I kept getting rejection letters that were kindly written, but each echoed the same sentiment: "We love this book. If you were already a published author, we would love to publish it." They were nice letters, but that didn't make the rejection any easier or the logic less frustrating.

Out of that came the audacious idea to start our own "publishing company." I put that in quotes because I want people to know a couple of things. First of all, we're not a traditional publishing company like most people envision when they hear the name. We don't have a printing press in our garage, and we don't have a marketing team. Basically, we're a middle-man who absorbs most of the front-end costs of publishing in order to help you get published, while making sure the majority of profits end up in your pocket, not ours.

Our desire is to keep costs to a bare minimum for each author. (As of this writing, there is only a minimal contract fee when your manuscript is accepted.) We provide resources and ideas to help authors work on marketing, while also providing the editor and graphic design artist at our expense. We subcontract out the printing, which speeds up the time it takes to move from final draft to bound book. Since we don't have much overhead we can keep our expenses low, allowing seasoned authors, or first-time authors like me, the opportunity to profit from their writing. This makes it possible for authors to publish more books while continuing in their current jobs or ministries.

Contact us
If you are interested in other books or learning about other authors from Overboard Books, please visit our website at www.overboardministries.com and click on the "Overboard Books" link. If you are an author interested in publishing with us, please visit our site and check out the "Authors" tab. There you will find a wealth of information that will help you understand the publishing process and how we might be a good fit for you. If we're not a fit for you, we'll gladly share anything we've learned that might be helpful to you as you pursue publishing through other means.

Thank you
Thanks for supporting our work and ministry. If you believe this book was helpful to you, tell someone about it! Or better yet, buy them a copy of their own! We completely depend on word-

of-mouth grassroots marketing to help spread the word about Overboard Ministries and its publications. Please share our website with others and encourage them to purchase the materials that will help them live "overboard" lives for Christ. Also be sure to visit our blog, easily accessible from the Overboard Ministries website, and while you're there sign up for our e-mail list.

May God bless you as you grab the side of the boat, take a deep breath…and jump onto the sea!

Joe Castañeda
Founder, Overboard Ministries
Lifer, Striving to live Overboard

Other Overboard Ministry Books

Project Joseph: **By Joe Castañeda**

Project Joseph was the first title published by Overboard Ministries. *Project Joseph* helps people walk through the pain of their past, using principles from the life of Joseph in Genesis, so that its readers can experience true healing from God. Many times it's our hurts and pains that keep us in the comfort of the boat instead of being on the water where Jesus is building His Kingdom. *Project Joseph* wants to help people heal so they can live their God-designed life on the water! Great for small group or individual study.

Dream House: **By Barry Bandara**

Dream House is all about marriage and family. Barry Bandara has written an excellent book, using the blueprint of a house, to guide readers into developing God-pleasing marriages and family. *Dream House* takes its readers on a room-by-room tour of a well designed home to illustrate the powerful principles of family and marriage laid out in God's Word. Another great Overboard title, perfect for small groups. (Pastors, this is an excellent book to base a preaching series on. Order copies for your congregation and then preach a series following the outline of the book. Makes a great one-two punch!)

Extreme Mind Makeover: **By Steve Etner**

Steve has written a very compelling book that challenges readers to apply God's Word to their way of thinking. Steve points out that everyday actions come from every-moment thinking, so if we want our actions to please God, we must start with God-pleasing thoughts. This book was forged out of Steve's personal journey and is a powerful tool filled with practical illustrations and loaded with Scripture. Learn to break bad habits and conquer sin with this book. Perfect for counselors.

Project Nehemiah: **By Joe Castañeda** *(March, 2012)*

Project Nehemiah is the second book by Joe Castañeda, and second in the "Life Improvement Series." Where *Project Joseph* was about looking back and trying to find healing for the pain of the past, *Project Nehemiah* is about looking forward to the plans of the future. By examining principles from the book of Nehemiah, this title will help readers understand how to tackle big projects for the Lord! *Project Nehemiah* is due to come out in March of 2012.

Overboard Ministries is growing and we are on the look-out for more exciting titles in 2012, and beyond! Work has already begun on three titles for the next year and contracts are being worked on with other authors. Be sure to check out www.overboardministries.com often, for the latest Overboard titles.

About the Cover

Nov 23, 2011

Joe, if you think the title text is not "grungy" enough, I understand and we can talk about it some more. Let me give a little explanation of what I'm thinking about overall design. One of the changes I made was to simplify and breakup the subtle background text, and, as a result, I was able to actually bring it out more and add to the overall grunge feel in the background. I also added the sparks flying that Steve suggested; great addition, I think.

Your suggestions were both very significant because they helped increase the contrast between (and actually develop) two major points of interest in this cover. I didn't even really have the contrast clearly in mind until thinking about this version of the cover. These are the concepts of EXTREME (i.e., dramatic process/God) and REAL LIFE (i.e., monochrome grunge/human).

The extreme concept (God's supernatural work in lives) is emphasized by color (gold), and cleaner lines, and angular strokes (sparks and sharper text, with lots of angles) while the messiness of real human/fallen life concept is symbolized by grunge in plainer brown tones.

This is just a way to look at the contrasts, which if a design is without it, will lack depth, richness, and meaning. Since the book is emphasizing dramatic change and dealing with real life issues (God vs. man), I think it is good to show some nice visual contrasts that relate to the concepts in the book.

I deviated away from the construction hammer concept we had talked about because when I was searching for hammer ideas, I ran into the hammer/anvil idea and forging steel. I thought that this concept has a lot of very good analogies to the extreme nature of making over a once shapeless mind, transforming it through heat, pressure, and pounding. Through that process, it is transformed into something it once wasn't, similar to the metamorphosis of a butterfly.

So the cover depicts primarily the process (in the blacksmith photo) and the result (in the butterfly silhouette) that is not always as prominent, but still a reality, using the rough, grunge-flavor background to give some sense of, again, the extreme and radical nature of change a mind must go through. This contrast is also analogous to the messiness of our lives as we go through the process of this change.

Nate Horton
www.igprodesign.com

Made in the USA
Charleston, SC
04 December 2012